ABOUT THE AUTHOR

Toronto-based Danko Jones has been singing and playing guitar in his eponymously named rock band for the last 20 years. In that time, his band has played in 37 countries on six continents and released 11 albums, three DVDs and over 30 music videos.

He has been writing for various rock publications around the world since 2005 and joined the KISS Army when he was six.

DANKO JONES

I'VE GOT SOME- THING TO SAY

Published by Feral House
1240 W Sims Way #124
Port Townsend WA 98368

www.feralhouse.com

ISBN: 9781627310574

Editing: Aaron Brophy
Foreword: Duff McKagan

Illustration credits:
p. 20–23: ©Gary Dumm
p. 32: ©Juan Montoya
p. 50–52: ©Mary Fleener
p. 60–63: ©Valient Himself
p. 70–71: ©Gary Taxali
p. 83–85: ©Michel "Away" Langevin
p. 93–94: ©Brian Walsby
p. 103: ©Damian Abraham
p. 111–113: ©Fiona Smyth
p. 139: ©Cam Hayden
p. 153: ©Eerie Von
p. 172: ©Richard Comely

Photo credits:
p. 10: Phil Lynott statue, ©Danko Jones
p. 121: Danko Jones & Robin Williams, ©Danko Jones
p. 129: The Ankh Warrior (4 images), ©Danko Jones

Design and typesetting: Ingrid Paulson
Cover art: Brian Walsby/Nick Sewell

TABLE OF CONTENTS

FOREWORD

Frankly stated, Danko Jones is one of my favourite people. Sure, sure . . . he is the hellhound, rebel-rousing rock 'n' roll singer we all see on stage (one hundred per cent that), but he is just so much more.

After hearing so much about the band Danko Jones, and being thankful to them for keeping the hard rock flag waving in the early oughts when everyone else was following some pretty awful trends, I finally got to meet Danko himself somewhere out on a tour in 2010 or so. He instantly struck me as the smartest guy in the room (any room), and it was apparent to me that one of his key strengths was his observational skills. You could tell he was watching and learning and mulling, but not judging.

And then I found out he was a writer. He was watching and learning . . . and getting material for his columns. Aha!

Humankind needs people like Danko. In his myriad reflections on culture, art, politics and people he perfectly articulates insights into everything from his own experiences that translate to a wider understanding of particular artists, being a gentleman, being a musician, working at a record store, or being on a tour bus, to what shouldn't be put on a hamburger. Oftentimes, it's not actually what Danko writes about, but how he writes about it. He writes as a well-travelled and cultured human being, shining a light for the rest of us.

I got to do a festival tour of Australia a couple years back with Danko. There was some sort of world-terror alert going on at this point, and as Danko and I were at airports every other day together I got to see some things from his viewpoint. Danko's style in dress is rather eye-catching to airport security I guess (oh . . . and he is browner than the average Australian), and at every security checkpoint, he'd be "randomly" selected for extra perusal. Now I was the observer, and what I saw in all of that turmoil and profiling was a calm man who could just shrug it all off and simply get on to the next rock show . . . unblemished and non-plussed.

I see the younger rock bands looking up to Danko now, and his podcasts have become stuff of legend. He is everywhere at all times, and he is always curious and well-informed. He writes it like he sees it, and we are all better for it. God Save Danko Jones!

Duff McKagan

Feb. 7, 2016

INTRODUCTION

I've never once considered myself a writer. I think "hack" is what would best describe me. I also know that always having *something* to say doesn't always mean that much. I'm merely a guy who has too many opinions on music and needs a healthy platform to get them out or else my insides will explode. Luckily my editors endure me patiently and I'm allowed to vomit judgement on Van Halen or Slayer or Ravi Shankar or hamburgers or feet. I'm convinced having this outlet has stemmed ulcers for years.

I don't know why I obsess over the minutiae of some bands. When you look at it objectively, it's a big waste of time. There are more pressing issues in the world than what album in a band's discography was best or why they should've done this or that. It's hollow barking, but goddammit it's a ton of fun.

Most of the ideas for these essays were birthed in dressing rooms, van rides, bus lounges and airport gates, where I'd engage either my bandmates, road crew, other bands or fellow rock fans in time-killing chitchat.

Any over-the-top adoration or inflamed criticism levelled at a band or person within these pages should be taken with a grain of salt. Hardline opinions may read like harsh criticism, but make no mistake, they're said out of pure fandom and utter devotion for the subject in question.

Remember, there are only two kinds of music—good and bad. Sometimes the good isn't all that great and sometimes the bad is fantastic.

Danko Jones

VIBING FOR THIN LIZZY

The derision that has been levelled at rock 'n' roll over the years has more to do with how it has presented itself than its music. In an effort to mirror its bombastic sound, like an annoying carnival barker yelling at a passersby, the genre has relied heavily on frivolous surface appearances, treating any sliver of substance as an afterthought.

To pre-teens, teenagers and the easily dazzled, the music doesn't need to be any deeper to find its mark. Lack of life experience isn't an obstacle when comprehending smoke bombs, pyro, laser light shows and flashy costumes. It's an easy sell that often treats the music secondary.

I can understand both sides of the fence. Being lured at an early age to rock 'n' roll through bands like KISS, Mötley Crüe and W.A.S.P., I was initially won over by their stage theatrics, wild make-up and scowling faces. Over time I found out that, unlike my other friends, I genuinely loved the music and stayed, enduring unending teasing by "cool" people who thought rock music was silly.

As much as I understood the music lacked depth, I revelled in it. I loved the too catchy choruses, ridiculous guitar solos and the puerile lyrics. Still, I wished there was a band that could bridge the gap and prove that this rock 'n' roll thing had substance without losing any of its sheen and bite.

Cue Thin Lizzy.

Thin Lizzy, hailing from Dublin, Ireland, upon first glance, seemingly lived every rock 'n' roll cliché one could find.

left: Making the pilgrimage to the Phil Lynott Statue on Harry St. in Dublin, Ireland. (2008)

These were conclusions made by those who only made cursory glimpses. When one looked longer and deeper, though, what they found was astounding—a band of immeasurable depth and emotion wading in this supposed shallow trough of rock music.

The crown jewel, of course, was lead singer/bassist and principal songwriter, Phil Lynott. Lynott, being of mixed race, didn't look like the quintessential rock star. With his lanky build and proud afro he was completely unlike rock poster boys of the time like Steven Tyler or David Lee Roth, but he harnessed an equal amount of magnetism. His songwriting went deeper than the standard "chicks 'n' drinks" crowd could understand. Songs like "Angel Of Death," "Got To Give It Up," "Black Boys On The Corner" and "Genocide" broached subjects that most rock bands didn't think about twice.

The music itself was beyond the usual "hack and slash" thump of their peers. Melody was paramount in every song but cleverly didn't fall prey to hackneyed pop drivel. A good heaping of their Irish heritage seeped into these songs along with the signature dual guitar interplay between whichever pair was at the helm, whether it was (Brian Robertson and Scott Gorham, Gorham and Gary Moore, Gorham and Snowy White, or Gorham and John Sykes).

Even if all of this failed to connect with an audience, what was undeniable was Lynott's voice. It remains one of the most recognizable in rock 'n' roll. It was Lynott's tone and timbre that simultaneously conveyed yearning, despair, heartache and honesty while managing to still remain cool and collected. It was a celestial voice heard once in a blue moon. Thank God he recorded it down onto tape for all of us to hear over and over again.

I must admit, as much as I was familiar with "Boys Are Back In Town" and "Jailbreak," I didn't pay them much mind growing up until I matured a bit. Once I felt the cruel sting of the real world, Lynott's voice and words began to sink in and make sense. When I had my heart broken for the first time, I realized Lynott was both the comforting painkiller and the warm shoulder I needed.

In all aspects of life, things that make profound impacts don't necessarily hit you over the head. They burrow and nestle; they're patient and subtle. And when they finally spread out, like the roots of a tree, they will reach further than you're even aware. As much as I love all the bands that grabbed me when I was younger, Lizzy's protracted embrace continues to burrow deeper within me every day.

A version of this piece was originally published in the
March 2015 issue of Rock Hard *magazine*

DON'T WORRY BE HAPPY = GLORIOUS SATANIC PRAISE

Metal is a perpetually maligned form of music. Its often Satanic over-tones have both attracted and perturbed people. It's been banned, picketed, ignored and laughed at for being "evil." Never has there been a music that has elicited such wide-ranging response. Which, when you think about it, is a testament to its weight as a cultural tour de force.

But while prudish gatekeepers have busied themselves trying to stop metal from being heard, blaming it for all sorts of ill-doings, I've often sat back and laughed at how misdirected these accusers have been.

It's quite simple. Ask yourself: what would Satan do? If you were Satan would you really back some loner dude in his mom's basement, wearing corpse paint, playing a gloomy keyboard and singing songs about you? Seriously, a lot of dudes who proclaim allegiance to Satan couldn't get laid if they were the only guy on a porno set, let alone convert new members over to Satanism. It would be like backing a gimp to run the Boston marathon. Satan isn't overlord of eternal hell for nothing. No, I think he's smarter than that.

If I were Satan and my goal was to convert as many souls as possible, I'd think big. Satan is the greatest sneak in the universe, smarter than Stephen Hawking to the power of a billion. So knowing this, wouldn't it make more sense for Satan to dwell within the grooves of musics that have more mass appeal?

The folly most so-called puritans make is only seeing what's immediately in front of them. For years, metal musicians have been accused of putting Satanic backward masking on records, but if I were Satan it would make way more sense to turn the tables around and hide sinister messages in pop records. I took five of popular culture's most beloved songs and played them backwards in hopes of finding equally evil messages and guess what? I found them. The results were downright bloodcurdling.

Let's take a look:

Bobby McFerrin "Don't Worry, Be Happy"
This feel-good song released in 1988 reached #1 on Billboard's Top 100 singles for two weeks, not to mention #1 in Canada, Germany, Australia and #2 in the U.K., Switzerland and Holland. But what almost everyone didn't realize is that, when spun backward, there is an unmistakable "Satan" spoken at the 32 second mark. Also, and this is the most mind-blowing, "Don't Worry" spun backward is "PARANOID"!! Try it for yourself. It's incredible.

R.E.M. "Shiny Happy People"
This 1991 single featuring The B-52's Kate Pierson qualifies as the most sung and equally mocked song. It's so happy it borders on sickening and peaked at #10 on Billboard. However, when you spin the song backward you distinctly hear "glory glory evil" at the 3:06 mark.

USA For Africa "We Are The World"
This charity single featuring the who's who of the American music industry in 1985 (Michael Jackson, Bruce Springsteen, Tina Turner, um, Dan Aykroyd) sold over 20 million copies and was the #1 single all over the world. However, when you spin the song backward you can distinctly hear "Lucifer's lonely" at the 6:49 mark.

Whitney Houston "The Greatest Love Of All"
Hitting #1 on Billboard's Top 100 in 1986, it was one of Houston's biggest hits. What people never realized was when it's spun backward one can hear "Satan rescuing me" at both the 53 second and 2:37 marks, respectively. At the 3:57 mark you can also hear "My friend whispers the good news."

The Beatles "All You Need Is Love"
Performed by The Beatles in the first ever live global television link and viewed by over 400 million people in 1967, the song was a worldwide #1 hit and remains one of the most recognizable tunes in pop culture. However, when you spin the chorus backward the line "all you need is love" comes out to "forgive me, lord" and the line "love is all you need" sounds like "give me Lucifer."

Sounds unbelievable? Go find the records and spin them backward yourself. It's very revealing how Satan has pervaded our society from a completely unexpected route, which, when you think about it, is exactly his way. No matter how long evil's been around, people still don't know where to go looking for it. It's hilarious and makes his job that much easier.

Satan's been evil long enough to figure out unbeatable ways for collecting damned souls. Maybe Christians figured out one of his methods (backward masking on records), but they failed to figure out where he would hide the true messages. Most of these dilettante Christians can't even operate a television remote control or check their own email let alone outsmart the emperor of all-evil.

Knowing this now, I'd suggest you watch your back when confronted with cute puppies, fresh flowers, sunny days and happy endings.

A version of this piece was originally published in the June 2013 issue of Close-Up Magazine

DENIM DEMONS UNITE!

When Arcade Fire won the Grammy for Album Of The Year in 2011, it was a historic and collective win for the Canadian music industry. Grammys are meant to recognize the best of the best in music and for that year our very own Arcade Fire bested everyone. But amidst the industry back-slapping and chants of "we're number one" from muso-journalists, I remained unusually quiet. You see, Grammy or no Grammy, while Arcade Fire are a damn good band, they're not the *best* band in the world. In fact, no matter what transitory trophy is presented to knight best band in the world, chances are they'll always get it wrong. You see, the best band in world aren't from Los Angeles or New York or London or Montreal. The best band in the world are from Oslo, Norway and they're called Turbonegro.

Back in 1998, while on tour with The New Bomb Turks, bassist Matt Reber and guitarist Jim Weber kept raving about this band they had just played with in Europe called Turbonegro. I immediately raised an eyebrow and interrupted with a "Turbo-What?" They played me their latest album *Apocalypse Dudes* and despite the sinister band photos of its six eyeliner wearing, fully bearded members, I chalked it up as a pretty darn good punk rock album but nothing more. Fast forward to 2002, standing amongst a rain-soaked crowd at the Hultsfred Festival in Sweden, I was getting ready to witness the Turbonegro reunion with their newly clean and sober singer Hank Von Helvete and I couldn't help but get caught up in the frenzy. When the band hit the stage, everything jigsawed into place like some death punk Keyser Söze. I instantly *got it* and my Turbonegro fandom increased exponentially.

Their 2003 return album *Scandinavian Leather* had them hitting the streets with a renewed vigour and garnered fans from as far and wide as Jello Biafra to James Hetfield. Their brand of punk rock, what they christened "death punk," was a homoerotic, biker/sailor, denim and leather goulash, with songs about prostitution, anal sex and . . . pizza. Think Alice Cooper meets The Ramones, or vice versa, with simple hooks and hummable melodies and you're getting close. But unlike The Ramones, Turbonegro's lyrical themes will have them banned from Starbucks outlets for a long time to come. Sure, Joey sang about sniffin' glue, but Turbonegro's most popular song is called "I Got Erection." Getting it now?

Years of touring abroad have made me aware of the wide dichotomy between the music tastes in North America and Europe. And while music pundits and punters alike have lined up to touch the hem of Justin Vernon's gown on this side of the Atlantic, Turbojugend, the worldwide fan club of Turbonegro, decked-out legions in the required denim jacket and sailor's caps, have lined the streets prostrated in reverence to the Sailor Men of Oslo everywhere else.

When I first met Turbonegro bassist Happy Tom (The Happy Sailor Man), he told me that "KISS have an army, but we have a navy!" He said it to me dead in the eye, fisting the air. It was irresistible. How do you not fall in love with a band after that? Of course, with original singer Hank Von Helvete having recently relinquished his spot as frontman only to be replaced by Tony "Duke Of Nothing" Sylvester on their supreme 2012 comeback record *Sexual Harassment,* the Norwegians are back in full force to vex and peeve. It should be noted that Helvete is one of the greatest frontmen that music has ever produced and I put him in the league that includes Iggy Pop, Paul Stanley, Axl Rose, Ozzy Osbourne and Lemmy Kilmister. His absence from the fold is gravely missed, but Turbonegro's sum parts are greater than their whole and trudge on they will.

It might sound cliché, but the one fast rule I always clung to when searching out music, throughout my teens and into adulthood was its requisite degree of danger. Whether it was KISS, Black Flag, *Motörhead*, Public Enemy, Diamanda Galas, Boredoms or John Coltrane's *Ascension*, to turn something as abstract as music into a scary happening was always attractive to me. But with the indie rock renaissance nowadays it just seems to me that everyone and their mom swallowed the blue pill in a Jim Jones/"Shiny Happy People"/*Little House On The Prairie* melt-down because they fear the truthbombs of songs like "Ace Of Spades," "Annihilate This Week" and "She Watch Channel Zero."

Over the years, it's only natural that my fandom for bands comes with diminishing returns. However, every so often there will come a band that will reignite that wide-eyed fervour I had when I was a teenager discovering music. I would venture to say that there's an even greater, or perhaps more desperate eagerness as I grow older and struggle to maintain this passion while everyone else around me seems to care less and less. Turbonegro are in that select group (that includes Grand Magus, Middle Class Rut, Shining (Norge), The Doomriders, Danava and Church Of Misery) that still make me *feel*. And as I watched them play with dropped jaw just this past Friday in Dortmund, Germany, and as I got ready to follow them on stage, I knew that the left-hand path that I had chosen was the correct one and I couldn't help but "Shake My Shit Machine."

Denim Demons, Unite! Remain Untamed! Darkness Forever!

A version of this piece originally appeared Nov. 9, 2012 on the Huffington Post *website*

BORN TO RAISE HELL

STORY BY DANKO JONES   ART BY GARY DUMM

ON DECEMBER 28, 2015, THE ROCK 'N' ROLL WORLD LOST ITS CAPTAIN WHEN LEMMY KILMISTER PASSED AWAY.

WE KNOW HOW TO DO IT AND WE DO IT REAL WELL...

WE ALL THOUGHT HE WAS GOING TO LIVE FOREVER. IT SURE SEEMED LIKE NOTHING COULD STOP HIM. LEMMY WAS THE FOUNDER, BASSIST AND SINGER OF THE LEGENDARY BAND MOTÖRHEAD, AND HE EMBODIED WHAT MANY OF US ASPIRED TO BE. HE DEFIED CONVENTION ALL WHILE LOOKING LIKE THE COOLEST CAT IN THE WORLD.

I'M VERY HAPPY I WAS ABLE TO MEET HIM AND THAT HE TOOK TO OUR BAND THE WAY HE DID...

...BRINGING US OUT ON TOUR, APPEARING IN OUR VIDEOS, LETTING ME SING WITH HIM ON STAGE. EVERY MINUTE I WAS IN HIS PRESENCE HELPED FULFILL THE ROCK 'N' ROLL DREAMS I HAD WHILE GROWING UP AND WANTING TO DO WHAT HE DID.

OUR BAND EMULATES A LOT OF WHAT MOTÖRHEAD STARTED AND CAME TO REPRESENT — MAXIMUM VOLUME AND POWER THROUGH MINIMUM SET-UP, BLACK-DRESSED FROM HEAD TO TOE, MELTING MUSICAL BARRIERS WITH AN EMPHASIS ON HEAVY. TO GET THE NOD FROM THE MAN WHO WAS THE ORIGINATOR IS AFFIRMING BEYOND BELIEF. EVERY TIME A SLING OR AN ARROW IS AIMED IN MY GENERAL DIRECTION, I USE LEMMY'S APPROVAL OF OUR BAND AS THE FORCEFIELD THAT PROTECTS ME FROM IT ALL.

I WANNA BURN IN HELL WITH YOU...

WHEN YOU WERE IN HIS PRESENCE HE WAS TOWERING AND IT WAS INTIMIDATING, TO SAY THE LEAST. HE STOOD SIX FEET-PLUS BUT YOU'D SWEAR HE WAS 10 FEET TALL. YOU WATCHED EVERY WORD YOU SAID AND DRANK UP EVERY WORD HE'D UTTER.

THE REVERENCE GIVEN TO HIM BY ALL WAS UN-MISTAKABLE AND EVEN IF YOU HAD NO CLUE OF WHAT A MOTÖRHEAD WAS, YOU KNEW HE WAS SOMEBODY. UPON MEETING HIM, ONE KNEW THIS RESPECT WAS WELL-EARNED, BUT ABOVE ALL ELSE, WELL-MAINTAINED BY HOW HE CARRIED HIMSELF — AS A GENTLEMAN TO ALL.

SO IMAGINE THE SPEED AT WHICH MY BOOTS WERE SHAKING ON NOVEMBER 10, 2008 ON TOUR IN GLASGOW, SCOTLAND WITH MOTÖRHEAD, WHEN GUITARIST PHIL CAMPBELL, CAME UP TO ME AND ASKED IF I WANTED TO SING THEIR SONG "BORN TO RAISE HELL" ON STAGE THAT NIGHT.

WANT TO SING IT?!

HELL YA!

I QUICKLY ACCEPTED. WHO IN THEIR RIGHT MIND WOULD TURN DOWN A CHANCE TO SING WITH THE MIGHTY MOTÖRHEAD, RIGHT? AND SINGING THE CHORUS? I'VE SUNG A CHORUS OR TWO BEFORE. "I GOT THIS" WAS WHAT I WALKED AWAY THINKING.

THAT'S NOT WHAT GOT MY BOOTS SHAKING. IT'S WHEN PHIL RETURNED AND ASKED ME TO DO ONE MORE THING.

LEM WANTS TO MAKE SURE YOU KNOW THE WHOLE SONG, SO MEET HIM IN HIS DRESSING ROOM AFTER SOUNDCHECK.

SHIT!

AS MUCH AS I WAS FAMILIAR WITH "BORN TO RAISE HELL," A SONG OFF THEIR 1994 ALBUM BASTARDS, WHICH FEATURED FEATURED WHITFIELD CRANE OF UGLY KID JOE AND THE ILLUSTRIOUS, ICE-T ON ONE VERSION, I DIDN'T EXACTLY KNOW THE LYRICS VERBATIM.

WHITFIELD CRANE

ICE - T

LET'S BE HONEST, I DON'T KNOW ALL THE LYRICS TO "ACE OF SPADES" EITHER AND TO LAY ALL MY CARDS OPENLY ON THE TABLE, I CAN'T REMEMBER HALF THE LYRICS TO MY OWN SONGS! SUDDENLY, I WAS GIVEN A LITTLE UNDER TWO HOURS TO LEARN THE LYRICS TO "BORN TO RAISE HELL" OFF-BY-HEART AND SING THEM BACK TO THE MAN WHO WROTE THE DAMN THING!

WHEN THE FATEFUL MOMENT ARRIVED, I MADE MY WAY TO LEMMY'S DRESSING ROOM LIKE A PRISONER WALKING THE PLANK.

LEMMY

I SAT DOWN ON A CHAIR ACROSS FROM HIM, HE PRESSED PLAY ON HIS IPOD AND WATCHED EVERY WORD COME OUT OF MY MOUTH, CHORUSES AND VERSES...

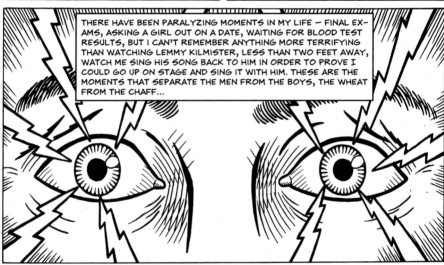

THERE HAVE BEEN PARALYZING MOMENTS IN MY LIFE — FINAL EXAMS, ASKING A GIRL OUT ON A DATE, WAITING FOR BLOOD TEST RESULTS, BUT I CAN'T REMEMBER ANYTHING MORE TERRIFYING THAN WATCHING LEMMY KILMISTER, LESS THAN TWO FEET AWAY, WATCH ME SING HIS SONG BACK TO HIM IN ORDER TO PROVE I COULD GO UP ON STAGE AND SING IT WITH HIM. THESE ARE THE MOMENTS THAT SEPARATE THE MEN FROM THE BOYS, THE WHEAT FROM THE CHAFF...

I SANG ON STAGE WITH MOTÖRHEAD THAT NIGHT.

...BORN TO RAISE HELL! BORN TO RAISE HELL!...

END

ROCK IS NOT DEAD

"Rock Is dead."

It's a statement that makes me shudder. Hearing it openly declared not only startles me as a fan, but disturbs me now that it has become my vocation. If nobody wants to hear it, who's gonna listen to the riffs that I write? If nobody wants to hear it, will there be anybody left to write riffs that will excite me?

This panic only lasts for a few moments, though. Until I remind myself we live in the internet age, where everybody now has a platform to pitch their uninformed opinions to an uninterested audience. So when someone carelessly posts "rock is finally dead" and I catch wind of it, I remind myself that it isn't written in stone, but rather a transitory, slapdash, bullshit remark meant only to drive online traffic toward whatever its source is peddling. Most of the time these quotes fail to gain any attention and fall by the wayside.

There is, however, one very specific instance when someone uttering the phrase "rock is finally dead" carried more weight than when it was written by a keyboard warrior thirsting for page views. Namely, the time it was uttered by Gene Simmons.

Gene Simmons, bassist/singer for the rock band KISS, despite being in the public eye for 40 years, has only recently risen to the coveted status of pop culture talking head. We can thank reality television and the perpetual need for online content that encourages people like Gene to talk continuously. He's savvy enough to know full well that the more sensational the statement, the hotter the spotlight. But the spotlight can eventually burn and his tendencies to provoke and prod have cost him dearly in the court of public opinion. His remarks on depression, immigrants, Islam, his open worship of money and his corny gloating over sexual conquests have done much to tarnish his image, leaving him even villainized to some.

When headlines started to emerge back in September of last year with Gene's proclamation in *Esquire* magazine that "rock is finally dead," the internet exploded with a giant middle finger pointed in his direction. People were lining up in droves to hurl their epithets at him before even reading the entire article. But when the dust settled and the kneejerk reactions faded from view, what we were seemingly left with was an innocuous, fatherly Gene extolling the new generation and lamenting their lot as have-nots.

Despite it being carefully crafted by the writer to make Gene look compassionate (the writer being Nick Simmons, Gene's son) and going so far as to insist he wasn't "an out-of-touch one-percenter" by name-dropping Tame Impala, it still came off more like a publicity stunt meant to improve Gene's dilapidated public persona rather than a genuine gesture of sympathy.

So delusional on the subjects he speaks about and unaware of the impressions he leaves, Gene goes so far as to blame the consumers, the fans themselves, for killing rock by downloading the music. He even blames the bands if they've engaged in downloading, too. This is classic ivory-tower-thinking—laying blame on what you see beneath you rather than looking around and above you.

If Gene was capable of applying critical thinking to his hasty thesis, he'd realize that it was in fact the record labels themselves who started this mess when they willingly introduced the liquid digital medium of compact discs into the marketplace. This was all motivated, not by the need to increase consumer value, but for the assurance of a boom period that lasted from the mid-1980s to the late-1990s, where almost overnight the record consumer was sold a bill of falsely inflated goods. Vinyl records costing $7.99 to $10.99 were stocked alongside their supposed audibly superior compact disc counterparts for $17.99 to $24.99. Catalogue titles went even higher, sometimes at $44.99 a pop.

Record company coffers filled to the brim as people scrambled to update their record collections and were basically swindled into re-buying what they already owned. When the industry introduced the word "remastered," they were able to sucker gullible dimwits a third time, but by then most of us caught on to the racket. As Gene is keen to point out in the Esquire article, the public decides what floats or fails with the placement of their dollar and to this day they've decided to hold on to their money so as to not get hoodwinked yet again by record labels.

But the most offensive idea he put forward in the article was his clumsy definition of rock music, assigning it validity and relevance only in direct relation to how many units it can move. If the art form in question fails to sell an amount comparable to past figures, it is, by Gene's assertion, dead. It's an arrogant and absurd notion to put forward, especially when the subject matter in question is still alive and arguably robust. Thinking like this diminishes rock music's worth and meaning, stripping it down to nothing but dollars and cents. These notions Gene puts forward are those of a village idiot.

While Gene prematurely announces rock's death, like some internet troll disseminating gossip about some wayward celebrity's false passing, others have taken it upon themselves to "save" it. Who better to assume the role than the Irish powerhouse quartet U2 fronted by their all-around Samaritan lead singer, Bono?

Bono's many charitable causes like his One foundation to fight global poverty and his (RED) charity to fight AIDS in Africa have been so widely praised it's threatened to overshadow his musical output. So when the music business is thrown into crisis and threatened to be dismantled, Bono seems like the only logical choice for saviour.

Never mind that his pleas to donate don't include his own band, considering they moved their publishing company to the Netherlands in

2006 to avoid the burden of paying taxes in their native Ireland—taxes that theoretically go back into the infrastructure and economy of their homeland. Never mind that Bono's private equity interests with Elevation Partners, who have invested in computer game companies like BioWare Corp. and Pandemic Studios that produce games like *Destroy All Humans 2* and *Mercenaries 2: World In Flames*, respectively, seem a tad contradictory to his humanitarian public face. And let us not forget U2's much publicized clash with SST Records in 1991 when Island Records sued the independent record label on behalf of the band after Negativeland released their *U2* EP—a move seen by many as an act of war against the independent spirit.

How did U2 attempt to save the music industry? By stealthily slipping their new album, *Songs Of Innocence* innocently onto unsuspecting iTunes accounts for free . . . without telling people kind of like how a vaccine contains the causative agent of the disease it's trying to prevent. Except in this case, it only caused more problems than it solved.

In one fell swoop and quite literally overnight, U2 turned the concept of the rock album into spam. However, unlike the spam you get on your computer telling you it will cure your erectile dysfunction, U2's album rendered rock albums flaccid. I wanted it off my computer as fast as I want those unwanted emails in my junk box folder containing trojan viruses. The argument can be made that incessant downloading had long rendered albums worthless, but by partnering up with iTunes, U2 not only became a culpable party, they made music "officially" worthless.

Downloading music "illegally" has never bothered me. It's an activity that keeps music lovers engaged with music, helping to create fanatics, aficionados and supporters that might not have had ready exposure or access otherwise. But when the creators themselves refuse to put a value on their output, that output instantly has no value. And much like a virus, this idea has now spread like wildfire, setting a dangerous example for others to follow.

Whether rock's monoliths (Gene and Bono) acknowledge it or not, they consciously or unconsciously seem to relish the idea of rock dying out. If this were indeed true and rock was to actually die, it would leave their respective legacies permanently uncontested and pristine, much like the ancient statues of emperors and their relics we see on television history shows.

Mirroring old empires, it was this bygone music industry that made stars out of Chaim Witz and Paul Hewson—better known as Gene Simmons and Bono, respectively. This is a music industry that seems alien by today's standards. When Gene declares rock's death, what he means, whether he realizes it or not, is the music industry that reared rock music as *he knew it* is dead. Even though he would have us believe the music industry was once a perfect system, one doesn't have to look too deeply to see its cracks and messes. I feel sorry for Gene in the same way one does when you see the aged grapple with their own mortality and the crushing reality of a world that's constantly changing.

Being in the music game for 18 years, all hope and excitement were quickly dashed after having every major and independent record label slam the door in our faces. Our band never got the courting or label-wooing other bands did. Thing is, the majority of those favoured bands have to open for us now. So much for A&R expertise. A lot of those A&R record label employees who laughed in our faces, never returned our calls and talked shit about our band are now selling used cars. So much for industry intuition and astuteness. We ended up aligning ourselves with a little punk rock label in Sweden (Bad Taste Records) who were told of us through another act on their label 15 years ago and whom we're still working with to this day. So much for a rock band's fickle dispositions.

Despite Gene's depiction of a music industry that nurtures and assists bands, being on the other side of the fence, I have a very different experience. And while one must not forget this delicate marriage of art and commerce inevitably yields to the dollars and cents, it also must acknowledge people's fragile dreams are being handled here. I have seen bands sign lopsided record deals and their careers stop instantly. I have seen bands with boundless potential crushed by some temporary expert telling them they had none. I will never forget when we sent a demo of songs to the president of a major label (that shall remain nameless) only to be told that she couldn't hear any "songs." We promptly took the same songs on that demo and toured the world with them. She ended up signing a rap-rock act that quickly broke up, so forgive me if I seem like I have an axe to grind . . . because I do.

Every time I hear about some record label employee who rejected our band getting demoted, dismissed or willfully leave the music biz, I smile. I smile, not because someone has lost their job, but because it's a quiet confirmation that we were right all along. I find it to be somewhat poetic justice when the impenetrable megalith that was the music industry, that churned out smug rock stars like Gene Simmons, was toppled by the tiny 15-year-old kids they tried to dupe into buying remastered compact discs. It's a modern day remake of the Pied Piper of Hamelin, only this time the piper's pipe came from the factory defective.

So, where does rock music go from here? I concede, most of the income generated from music these days, and consequently funnelled back in, comes from other genres like pop music (Beyonce, Katy Perry, Lady Gaga), indie rock (Arcade Fire, Mumford & Sons), electronica (Skrillex, Deadmau5) and rap (Jay Z, Kanye West, Drake) so it makes it harder for rock bands to get prioritized for things like tour support, recording budgets and much-needed marketing money from labels. Nightmarish 360 deals, whereby a label takes more ownership of a band (i.e. merchandising and live concert guarantees) has reared its unavoidable head, too.

Still, rock hasn't died so much as its playing field has been levelled. Now everyone has an almost equal chance to be heard. The new Audrey Horne album got to my ears quicker than the new AC/DC album did this year. I heard the new Pallbearer before I even heard Judas Priest had released a new album. And the reason is that I am susceptible to the strongest form of marketing out there—word of mouth. People informed me, through blogs, Twitter, Instagram, hanging out with friends and music magazines.

Even though rock music is well past its glory days, supplanted by more modern sounds, it continues to survive on like a cockroach, ebbing and flowing depending on the musical tide, but never dying. And while I do get nervous hearing that it has yet again been pronounced dead on arrival, there's a side of me that takes pleasure from it being so hastily eulogized. When freed from the burden of needing to be relevant and alive, rock music can rattle around making noise in the background, free to draw breath far away from self-appointed pundits' judgements, their imposing confines and warped interpretations.

People like Gene assign relevance only to what is directly in front of them—a cloudy top-shelf view of the world. What is it with the American directive to only place relevance and import on things classified as "number one"? It's terribly frustrating, like insisting on eating only the icing on a cake without trying what's underneath; sooner or later you're gonna get sick. We all know what "number one" is because the top of the mountain is the easiest thing to see, but those of us with voracious musical appetites want to explore so much more. I want to hear "number two," "number three," all the way down to "number 1,000". And I'm damn sure I'm not the only one.

Let's make one thing very clear: there is no "death" here. There is no mourning needed. Nothing has died. Nothing is in danger of disappearing. In fact, when I hear bands like Admiral Sir Cloudesley Shovell, Broken Teeth, Mos Generator, The Biters, Giuda, Biblical and The Night Flight Orchestra, I know rock is as active and buoyant as ever. But if people insist on rock being dead then let them mourn its passing. Let them move on with their lives and find new interests to pass their time. Let the pop stars of today flood the marketplace. Let the indie rock heroes coddle everybody. Let electronica luminaries numb its hordes. Let the rappers overload demand. Let's allow rock to go the way of jazz, complete with obligatory nods to its existence and be done with it.

Rock music is not a music to represent the masses anymore. It's been kicked and beaten down, unquestionably the result of overexposure, kind of like when wine gets "corked" (who needs to hear "Stairway To Heaven" ever again?). However, it now wears its scars on its sleeves and has become darker, more sinister and less vulnerable to bullshit.

Sure it comes with baggage, but it yields to no one. It's hardened, just like it's supposed to sound, and it's glorious.

This is a gestation period for rock; a time where it's meant for only those who love it and watch over it. Rock music should fade from the foreground, slip into the underground and reclaim its rightful outsider status. Its deserved place should be in the shadows.

A version of this piece was originally published in the February 2015 issue of Visions *magazine*

THE KISS RYB COLOUR WHEEL

On September 18, 1978, each member of KISS simultaneously released a solo album. It was an achievement no other band had done before or since. While all bets were riding on Paul Stanley's or Gene Simmon's albums to be the most successful, everyone was surprised when guitarist Ace Frehley quietly fared the best when he scored a genuine hit with his Russ Ballard remake of "New York Groove" reaching #13 on Billboard charts. Although all four albums eventually went platinum, no one was prepared for the schism that ripped the KISS Army asunder. You still can't talk to a KISS fan without delving into their favourite KISS solo album which inevitably breaks down into which member is their favourite and why.

One of the most distinguishing features of the four albums, and quietly one of the main dividing lines within the band, lay in the fantastic and now iconic portraits by Eraldo Carugati that graced each solo album. Since various tensions between band members have long been publicly aired, one can see how Carugati's colour choices came to subtly mirror their various in-band dynamics. It's almost a case of which came first: a subconscious response by each member to behave according to each's assigned Carugati colour, or Carugati's almost psychic ability to read each member's aura?

First, let's take a look at the colours Carugati chose and the relationships between each one. Assuming he went by this RYB model, the first indication of a divide between members is here at colour assignment. In colour theory, there are two models one can use to describe how colours are sequenced. Most painters go by what is referred to as an RYB colour model used for mixing paints together—Red, Yellow and Blue as primary colours and Violet, Orange and Green are secondary colours. Primary colours were delegated to Gene Simmons (Red) and Ace Frehley (Blue) while Paul Stanley (Violet) and Peter Criss (Green) were given secondary colours. This designation doesn't outwardly mean anything other than illustrating how one solves working with a four-piece rock band and having to assign signature looks using two separate colour triads. It's merely a way of fitting a circle into a square peg.

Upon first glance at the RYB colour wheel, one can't help but notice that Carugati's appointed colours mirror the actual KISS front-of-stage plot when the colour Violet (Paul) is placed at the top of the model, front and centre, flanked by Red (Gene) on its right side and Blue (Ace) on its left side. Knowing that each colour has its own corresponding opposite colour (also known as its complementary colour), more discernible patterns come to light when the wheel is spun to feature Red (Gene) on top revealing Green (Peter) as its opposite on the bottom. It's in this position where the colours start mirroring each member's group status. It's no secret that Gene's image has been used by outside sources as the go-to representative of the band, not to mention his governing hand over the KISS empire with Paul on his right-hand side, as accurately displayed on the wheel itself. Peter is on the bottom with Green, which can only mean as the first of the original four to leave the group, he's the furthest from the epicenter (Gene). Sandwiched next to Green (Peter) and Violet (Paul) sits Blue (Ace) as Ace Frehley was the next member to leave the band.

It's also interesting that Carugati chose to use the half-side of the colour wheel—Red to Red Violet all the way down to Blue Green and Green— that colour theory describes as "cool," in order to not let any colour override the larger-than-life subject matter. The variance between colours can be designated into these two camps by describing colours as either warm or cool. Warm colours tend to excite and run from red to yellow, whereas cool colours are placid and run from red to green. It is also argued that choosing to pair colours that lie parallel on the colour wheel is more aesthetically pleasing. Say what you will about colour theory and this aspect of it, but it's undeniable the calming effect one gets when looking at each album cover, even when Gene's demon face is staring at you with blood seeping from his lips.

It should also be noted here that Carugati employed the filmic technique of backlighting each member with respective hues. Backlight is popular in film because it always seems to make whatever subject matter more prominent. It's what made Marlene Dietrich and Greta Garbo even more beautiful. In this instance, when dealing with KISS members, let's just describe the resulting covers as "alluring."

Let's look at how:

Gene Simmons: Spitting blood and breathing fire, it's simple to ascribe the colour Red to The Demon. Traditionally, Red has represented everything from blood and hell to lust and love. Gene has done much to toy with all shades the colour represents, both onstage and offstage. Whether it's flirtatiously flicking his long tongue in between bass lines or tastelessly boasting that he has slept with over 2,000 women, Gene embodies the attributes that Red reflects. His place as the top arc on the KISS version of the RYB colour wheel doesn't go unnoticed since he lords over the band's business.

Ace Frehley: As The Spaceman, Ace is very appropriately swathed in Blue. Remember, these portraits were made in 1978, just six years after the first colour images of Earth were released, which NASA dubbed "The Blue Marble." Back then, Blue was most certainly associated with space. On the KISS RYB colour star Blue (Ace) sits between Green (Peter) and Violet (Paul), the second farthest from Red's (Gene) group dominance and fittingly Ace was second of the four to leave the group. Perhaps it's no coincidence that Ace later admitted to feeling closest to Peter.

Paul Stanley: Assigning Violet to Paul was a perfect choice. It's a mix between Red (Gene) and Blue (Ace), mirroring Paul's centre stage positioning. As a singer/guitarist/frontman, Paul is a mixture of both—fantastic showman with a musical proficiency second to none. Purple, a shade of Violet (between Violet and Red) is also the colour of nobility, which Paul seems to embody as the ambiguous "Starchild" character. The designation of Violet on the KISS RYB colour wheel sits harmoniously parallel to Red (Gene), indicative of the duo's long-standing partnership.

Peter Criss: Green is a complicated colour and culturally has contradictory meanings. Green represents nature and rebirth associated with the environmental "green" movement, which is completely opposite of Red's destructive tendencies and makes sense with Criss' "Cat" persona. But it also can mean envy and sickness. These opposing forces for Green existed within Criss as well. As a drummer who could sing, and arguably quite well, Criss yearned for the center stage, which he eventually wrangled when he left the band only to fail miserably. "Beth," his most famous KISS song, stands almost directly opposite the band's hard rockin' prime directive.

Characters like The Green Goblin, Doctor Octopus, Mysterio and Electro were all deliberately cast in Green opposite Spider-Man's dominant Red. In KISStory, these same forces are at work, especially between Simmons and Criss. Gene is Jewish, an only child raised in Queens, New York by a single mother, while Peter is Italian-Catholic, oldest of five children raised in Brooklyn. While Gene named himself in tribute after rockabilly singer Jumpin' Gene Simmons, Peter loved jazz and studied under Gene Krupa. As the first of the original four members to leave the band, it's now generally known that Criss struggled with drugs, but also with Simmons who presided over the power structure within.

Moreover, Gene has also drawn a lot of controversy in recent years for his outspoken remarks on Islam and, although this observation may be going out on a limb, Green just happens to be a sacred colour in Islam. Even the flag of Hamas is predominantly Green. It's a touchy subject that back in 1978 Carugati could have had no idea he was tinkering with when he innocently assigned each member their colour.

When it was all played out and all the dust had settled, the albums assigned with primary colours in the RYB colour wheel—Red and Blue—fared the best on the Billboard charts with Gene's record peaking at #22 and Ace's peaking at #26. Paul and Peter's albums, assigned with secondary colours, peaked at #40 and #43, respectively. Perhaps it was an intuitive connection to the colour spectrum that led fans to subconsciously sequence the success of each solo album.

As a lifetime member of the KISS Army, these colour designations and interpretations are probably only noticeable to me. I know I'm not to be trusted since I can glean spiritually fulfilling significance from "Lick It Up," find hidden meaning combing through the lyrics of "Love Gun" and decode some numerical congruence between the songs on *Crazy Nights*. In other words, yes, I'm a doofus.

A version of this piece was originally published in the October 2011 issue of Close-Up Magazine. *Illustration by Juan Montoya*

DUNGEONS AND HEAVY METAL AND DRAGONS

In order to brand someone a complete loser, I've often described people as avid fans of Dungeons & Dragons. Dungeons & Dragons is a role-playing dice game where players are assigned a character and embark on journeys battling fantastic creatures for power and treasure through the luck of the dice. It's very much like the *Lord Of The Rings* series come to life, except you do it on your dining room table with pens, pencils, dice, your imagination and a bunch of other guys with nothing else to do on a Friday night. It's a game that is geek approved and only geeks play it. I've used this cliché when I've wantonly put people down and I've done it within the pages of *Close-Up Magazine*. I've snickered when I've written it and laughed out loud when I read it back. Why? Because when it comes to Dungeons & Dragons all the clichés are true.

You only have time to play this life-devouring game if you've got nothing better to do, are unemployable, not getting laid on a regular basis, never ever gotten laid, never will get laid, will never get laid in your next life, or all of the above. There isn't enough space within these pages to describe the parade of rejects who are attracted to this game. But you do not find the game: the game finds you.

I've often thought about my malicious comments aimed at D&D and worried that people may begin to suspect he "doth protest too much." If you've ever thought the same after reading one of my personal and off-topic harangues then you've figured out the truth—I *love* Dungeons & Dragons. Yes, it's been my dirty little secret all these years. OK, I'll wait until you finish laughing . . . as I was saying, it's been my dirty little secret and one I've kept hidden for obvious reasons.

I've grappled with this dilemma for quite a while now. Each time I put down other gamers I felt a dishonest, hypocritical sting. It's a similar feeling to when the nerd in the high school joins the cool jocks and cheerleaders in every 1980s teen coming-of-age comedy movie. In this case, the cool kids were actually *Close-Up* readers (go figure?).

The connection shouldn't be that much of a surprise. After all, metal has a lot in common with Dungeons & Dragons when it comes to imagery and lyrical content. I don't know who owes whom residual cheques—Iron Maiden's Steve Harris to TSR Games (the ol' Dungeons & Dragons people) or vice versa? Either way, there's no denying the link between the two. But most people who play D&D, at least the ones I've been able to meet, aren't even metal fans. And most metal fans laugh when you even hint at D&D.

As an avid gamer and reluctant Dungeon Master*, I try to incorporate a metallic edge to each campaign by acting as deejay throughout the evening. I find it lends to the mood and punches up each player's role-playing. As Dungeon Master your job is to describe the action and create the story, so what better an aid than music? Often too, by the campaign's end, most people, who weren't fans before, leave with a new list of albums to track down. Sure, there's more effort in incorporating music into one's Dungeon Master-ing, but with today's technology you can easily turn a humdrum night of D&D into a splatter-filled romp of dragon slaying and guitar wailing.

Much has changed in the D&D universe over the years with the expansion of classes and inclusion of new races through the TSR to Wizards Of The Coast eras, and although these updates have been widely praised, my compadres and I prefer the TSR/Gary Gygax AD&D edition.

---

* Dungeon Master (DM) – The omnipotent overlord of every Dungeons & Dragons campaign. It is the Dungeon Master who determines the pace and the feel of each game.

The following is a quick primer to make your D&D campaign more exciting *and* more metallic. Please remember these are rules adhering to my paradigm. Use it only as reference and proceed as you wish.

SETTING THE TONE
Conducting my campaigns usually means the DM also becomes the DJ. Being the omnipotent master of the players' fantasy world means controlling the pace and tone of gameplay, and music has a large part in that. In order to do this effectively I use the DJ 1800 for Mac, which turns my laptop into a DJ console, complete with mixer. It emulates the Denon DN 1800F self-contained DJ professional system and it's fabulous. I will confess here and say a great deal of preparation is needed to have it effectively improve gameplay, but when done correctly, it's the closest thing to actually picking up a sword yourself.

CHARACTER THEMES
When players create their characters, I allow for individual theme music. Although this can be a technical nightmare, I allow each character to be represented audibly by a certain group or musician's selected discography. These selections should be carefully made because it will remain throughout the campaign, or at least until they reach the next level. Dungeon Masters should be very stringent when allowing "Character Themes" and never allow music outside the realm of D&D. For example, allowing a character to be represented by AC/DC, Van Halen or even some Bay Area thrash band, regardless of character class, is a flagrant disregard for what is realistically representative in the D&D realm. If "Highway To Hell" or "I'm The Man" can be played every time a player's turn is up, how does the tone differ from playing Robotech, Top Secret or even Monopoly? There are requirements to be met in choosing music to every aspect of a D&D campaign. Such as . . .

i) Character Classes
A player's character class is more than just their profession or job; it's their calling. There are seven character classes in the AD&D edition (Magic-User,

Fighter, Dwarf, Elf, Halfling, Cleric, Thief) and just how each class has specific things they can use when it comes to weapons, armour, magic abilities, so do these same rules apply to music. Common sense is my only compass when incorporating music. For example: a Fighter can use the music of Saxon, Dio or Iron Maiden through his/her rise through the first to third levels, but as the experience points rack up, the music may graduate to Hammerfall, Armored Saint or Amon Amarth. The same goes with a Magic-User, initially using the music of Dio, but slowly graduating to Opeth and Blackmore's Night.

HEAVY METAL BY CHARACTER CLASS

CLERIC

LEVEL	GROUP 1	GROUP 2	GROUP 3	GROUP 4	GROUP 5
1	Iron Maiden				
2–3	Iron Maiden	Candlemass			
4–6	Iron Maiden	Candlemass	Cathedral		
7–9	Iron Maiden	Candlemass	Cathedral	Opeth	
10	Iron Maiden	Candlemass	Cathedral	Opeth	Blackmore's Night

FIGHTER

LEVEL	GROUP 1	GROUP 2	GROUP 3	GROUP 4	GROUP 5
1	Dio				
2–3	Dio	Saxon			
4–6	Dio	Saxon	Hammerfall		
7–9	Dio	Saxon	Hammerfall	Manowar	
10	Dio	Saxon	Hammerfall	Manowar	Amon Amarth

THIEF

LEVEL	GROUP 1	GROUP 2	GROUP 3	GROUP 4	GROUP 5
1	Dio				
2–3	Dio	Satyricon			
4–6	Dio	Satyricon	Cult Of Luna		
7–9	Dio	Satyricon	Cult Of Luna	Earth	
10	Dio	Satyricon	Cult Of Luna	Earth	Emperor

ii) Character Alignment & Black Metal

A character's choice of alignment represents the morals and principles they consciously decide to live by. A lot of players enjoy role-playing with characters of a darker alignment. Characters that are Chaotic Evil or Lawful Evil just seem to be more fun than characters who are simply Lawful Good. Clerics I've played with indulge themselves by worshipping sinister demons, acting erratically and generally behaving foolishly. Sometimes it can slow gameplay, but rarely does it get boring.

When incorporating black metal make very sure the kind of black metal you are using correlates with a character's alignment. For example, a Chaotic Evil Fighter may definitely have access to Immortal, but cannot even dare incorporate the music of Emperor or Nachtmystium. While Neutral Evil Magic Users and Clerics can use Enslaved, it's almost ludicrous to intimate the usage of Carpathian Forest or Cradle Of Filth. Why bother incorporating the delicate and sensitive genre of black metal if you're not going to adhere to its, albeit somewhat hypocritical, sense of order? If this all seems a little too complicated, and dare I say cliquey, may I suggest avoiding black metal entirely and sticking to your regular fare of chaotic and lawful evil bands like Celtic Frost, Venom, Deicide, Slayer and Morbid Angel.

CAMPAIGN & COMBAT

As stated earlier, your job as DM is to create the mood, describe the action and tell the story during the campaign. No time is music more vital than during the minute-by-minute action of the campaign, especially during combat. It is a good idea to have a prepared playlist filled with tunes for the melee. I like to keep a loop of various playlists that I make up days and sometimes weeks before game day (which over time have accumulated to a nice collection I can summon at my fingertips). More meticulous DMs can go from song to song determined by how the campaign is faring, but good luck trying to keep that all in order (believe me, I've tried). For example, a tedious tromp through a magical forest can be accompanied by some nauseating Enya, sinister Sunn0)))) or dried-out Sarah McLachlan, but how do you make a quick transition if the dice reveal a giant centipede starting a spontaneous fracas? Are your fingers as fast as your head to make the transition to some good ol' Saxon?

Example of Play

Jfaiffer is a third-level Fighter. He currently uses "Sunset Superman" by Dio as his theme.

Moldar is a second-level Cleric. He currently uses "Under The Oak" by Candlemass as his theme.

Serpena is a third-level Magic User. She currently uses "Quest For Fire" by Iron Maiden as her theme.

DM is playing "Mr. Peagram's Morris And Sword" by Blackmore's Night.

DM: At the end of the field you see what looks like the opening of a forest.

Jfaiffer: Let's walk towards it.

Moldar: No, wait, from afar, what overall colour is the forest?

DM: It has a dark blue hue.

Moldar: OK, fuck that, let's NOT go in there. It's too dangerous.

Jfaiffer: I'm going and I'm running towards it.

DM rolls for random monsters due to Jfaiffer's boisterous running while playing "Soldiers Of The Wasteland" by Dragonforce.

DM: OK, Jfaiffer, you've awakened a giant rat and he's ready to attack you.

Jfaiffer: Ahhhh!

Serpena: See, Jfaiffer you have to listen to Moldar more often.

Jfaiffer: Fuck Moldar and fuck that giant rat. Let's go for it!

DM plays "Nattfodd" by Finntroll during the ensuing melee.

DM and Jfaiffer roll initiative. DM rolls a 5 and Jfaiffer rolls a 6. Jfaiffer attacks first.

Jfaiffer: Attacking with my two-handed sword.

Jfaiffer rolls an 11 from a 20-sided dice (1d20) and with the Rat's AC (armor class) being 9, his attack finds a mark. Rolling for hit point damage, it's a straight 6 again. The Rat has 4 hit points and dies instantly.

DM plays Jfaiffer's theme "Sunset Superman" by Dio at the end of the fight.

Serpena: Close call Jfaiffer.

Jfaiffer: There are never any close calls for Jfaiffer! Only assured DEATH!

DM: OK gang, do you still proceed into the forest? There is another route over the mountains, but I'm just telling you now that there are too many monsters for the three of you and little reward. The forest is dangerous as well, but there is enough treasure and opportunity to raise your levels by the time you're through.

Moldar: I guess we proceed into the forest.

Jfaiffer: I'm running in!

Serpena: Wait!

DM: Jfaiffer, I wouldn't do that if I were you!!!!!

Jfaiffer has a +1 protective modifier while his theme song is playing and a +1 bonus because it's Dio. (My campaigns always include a +1 bonus modifier on roles when Dio and Saxon are playing.) Which brings us to . . .

DIO & IRON MAIDEN

These are two staple bands that really require no introduction. With Dio's recent passing, his music has taken a slightly more melancholic, almost crestfallen tone when played during campaigns. At least, that's how it feels to me. Both bands are quite possibly the most versatile in the world of D&D. Both Magic-Users and Fighters can use them and their music is also interspecies friendly with Dwarves curiously using Dio most often. Depending on the situation, Maiden's music is almost synonymous with the game itself and can be used for almost any class with almost any alignment. There have been nights spent with ceaseless marathons of Dio and Maiden accompanying dice rolling through petrifying mazes and eerie caverns for both characters and my own DM playlist. Nothing beats campaigning through a hollowed-out Egyptian grave with Clerics and Thieves while having Iron Maiden's "Powerslave" on full blast.

Here's an example of how a character's theme song use can progress through a campaign:

FIGHTER EXPERIENCE TABLE USING IRON MAIDEN

LEVEL	TITLE	EXPERIENCE POINTS	THEME SONG
1	Myrmidon	0	Duellists
2	Veteran	2000	Invaders
3	Swordmaster	4000	Stranger In A Strange Land
4	Hero	8000	Running Free
5	Swashbuckler	16000	2 Minutes To Midnight
6	Warrior	32000	Sun And Steel
7	Champion	64000	Flash Of The Blade
8	Superhero	120000	The Trooper
9	Lord	240000	Killers

MAGIC USER EXPERIENCE TABLE USING IRON MAIDEN

LEVEL	TITLE	EXPERIENCE POINTS	THEME SONG
1	Medium	0	The Ides Of March
2	Seer	2500	Déjà vu
3	Conjurer	5000	Quest For Fire
4	Magician	10000	Can I Play With Madness?
5	Enchanter	20000	Children Of The Damned
6	Warlock	40000	Powerslave
7	Sorcerer	80000	The Clairvoyant
8	Necromancer	160000	Flight Of Icarus
9	Wizard	320000	Hallowed Be Thy Name

REWARDS & BONUSES

When ability scores are high enough, I usually allow bonus songs during an individual's turn. For example, guiding a fifth-level Thief with a Dexterity score of 19 or higher, (in keeping with that class' prime requisite) utilizing Celtic Frost's "Into Crypts Of Rays" as their theme, they might be allowed to play "Babylon Fell" every now and then while never overriding the DM's omnipotent role of setting the overall musical tone. When more than one character in a campaign have high ability scores it can get messy. As DM I end up giving out musical related rewards piecemeal or letting the players bring their own iPod and plugging into the stereo system.

When a character gains enough experience points to reach the next level, I usually reward the player with a song of my choosing. For example, a tenth-level Fighter that becomes an eleventh-level Fighter during a round might get a sudden spin of "Warrior" by Saxon off the *Power & Glory* album, just for kicks. Hey, the onus is on you to keep AD&D fun first and foremost for everyone, including yourself.

Dungeons & Dragons is a slippery slope to climb if you insist on strictly abiding by the rules with little leeway. Every "rule" I've laid out here is merely suggestions and examples of how friends and I make gameplay fun by incorporating the gameplay world with the heavy metal world. As much as heavy metal raucously spruces up an already festive night of dice rolling and role-playing, so does Dungeons & Dragons leave its imprint on the music by making fantastical lyrics and brawny riffs sparkle with spirit.

A version of this piece was originally published in the October 2010 issue of Close-Up Magazine

THERE'S NO SUCH THING AS A MUSICAL GUILTY PLEASURE

Having done my fair share of interviews over the years, here are three questions I can't stand:

1) How do you guys write your songs?
2) Do you like playing festivals or clubs more?
3) Do you have any guilty pleasures?

The first two questions are benign queries that are usually employed by music journalists to conceal their lack of research, lack of interest or lack of interview skills. Either way, I always answer politely and get ready for the next set of vapid questions. I'm fully aware how much a privilege it is to have someone take time out of their own life to ask questions, insipid or not, about you and your life. I know I could be doing a lot worse and never take it for granted, but it's the third question of the group that has me biting my tongue in order to keep from lashing out.

I detest the term "guilty pleasure."

Guilty pleasure, when applied to music, means music that you can only listen to in secret because it hasn't been deemed "cool" enough by self-appointed music gatekeepers. It's a term most likely coined by A&R

reps at major label companies because they've always been the ones at the club who constantly look around, particularly at other A&R reps, to see if they too should like whatever's being watched. Sadly, this habit has now been embraced by scores of wannabe aficionados too clueless to judge for themselves.

When a music is tagged as a "guilty pleasure" it's viewed as socially unacceptable. It also happens to bring down the pastime of music listening to a high school cliquish level . . . except it involves supposedly grown adults. People who actually feel guilty listening to certain musics are the same people who picked on you in high school, screw in the missionary position with a three-stroke maximum and need a laugh track when watching comedy to prompt them when to guffaw. They also don't know what "guffaw" means.

Many people use one's musical tastes as a sieve for finding like-minded individuals and harshly judging others whose tastes don't correspond. It's a practice that assumes the direction in which one's ear bends is in direct correlation with one's quality of character. Of course, it only takes two minutes to realize that these rationalizations are based on some juvenile nonsense.

And who is making up these rules for discerning taste? From my observation, just like in high school, there are style-bullies who preside over what gets deemed "cool." And in the weirdest *Twilight Zone* episode ever, the same kind of people who used to wear varsity letterman jackets, throw footballs around and wear lacrosse shirts have now traded it all in for pork pie hats, ironic Rollie Fingers/Mr. Monopoly moustaches and calabash pipes in a desperate bid to look distinguished. They only succeed in looking like assholes.

You like Justin Timberlake and Kanye West while the rest of your friends listen to The Lumineers or the Yeah Yeah Yeahs? You like Nachtmystium and Watain, but your buddies like The Black Keys and Fun.? You like AC/DC and Katy Perry, but your co-workers like Wolf Eyes and NOFX?

Who gives a shit?

Rock 'n' roll or whatever you want to call this always hinged on deviance. When I start to detect a set of rules being implemented by these numbskull moderators, I knee-jerk into my true asshole-self and thumb my nose at their stipulations. Over the years, our band has paid dearly for stubbornly sticking to our hard rock stylings instead of trend-hopping, subsequently inviting the slings of johnny cum-lately hepcats everywhere. It's been a small price to pay to be able to look at yourself in the mirror each morning.

So exactly what music should you listen to? It all depends on what circle you want to join. These types of condescending overlords exist in every scene, office space, social clique. The only guilty pleasure that should be shamed, if exposed, are these tastemaking, gate-keeping bullies and their need to cover up their own self-doubt.

Danko Jones
Proud fan of Billy Joel, Danzig, Polvo,
Scorpions, Kylie Minogue, Ice-T,
The Gories, George Michael, The
Doomriders, Fugazi, Wu-Tang Clan,
Manowar and Bruno Mars

A version of this piece originally appeared May 4,
2013 on the Huffington Post *website*

I'M SICK OF SEEING YOUR DISGUSTING FEET!!

MOST OF US, IF WE COULD, WOULD CHANGE AT LEAST ONE THING ABOUT OURSELVES. I'M GUESSING THE MOST COMMON CHANGES WOULD BE...

WEIGHT LOSS · FACIAL RECONSTRUCTION · INCREASED PENIS SIZE

DOES THIS MAKE ME LOOK FAT?

INCREASED BREAST SIZE, "SELFIE"

CENSORED!

...AND REVERSAL OF HAIR LOSS.

HEY!

WITH THE EXCEPTION OF PENIS SIZE, ALL THESE CHANGES OCCUR ABOVE THE WAIST BECAUSE WE DO MOST OF OUR INTERACTING WITH EACH OTHER FROM THE WAIST UP.

NICE SMILE · EVERYTHING IS NICE · COOL CLOTHES · BLAH BLAH BLAH BL · CUTE NOSE · BLAH BLAH · BLAH BLAH · BLAH BLAH · BLAH BLAH BL BLAH · BLAH BLAH BLAH · BLAH BLAH BLAH · BLAH BLAH BLAH · BLAH BL BLAH · BLAH BL BLAH · BLAH BLAH · BLAH BLA BLAH B

STILL, THERE'S ONE BODY PART WHICH DOESN'T GET ENOUGH ATTENTION SINCE IT'S LOCATED WAY BELOW AND FAR FROM IMMEDIATE SCRUTINY.

IN MY HUMBLE, POLITICALLY INCORRECT OPINION, MOST PEOPLE SHOULD SERIOUSLY CONSIDER GETTING A BRAND NEW PAIR OF FEET!!!

LIVING IN THE COLD CLIMATE OF CANADA KEEPS OUR FEET TIGHTLY COCOONED IN BOOTS and SHOES FOR MOST OF THE YEAR.

BUT IT'S THESE LONG WINTER MONTHS THAT MAKE MOST CANADIANS YEARN TO DISROBE AT THE FIRST SIGN OF ABOVE-FREEZING TEMPERATURES.

WHAT INEVITABLY HAPPENS AFTER THE 1ST SNOW MELT OF THE YEAR IS AN IMPROMPTU STREET PARADE OF BARELY CLAD PEDESTRIANS SUDDENLY FREED FROM THE SHACKLES OF PARKAS, LONG JOHNS, TOQUES, and GLOVES.

TEXT: DANKO JONES　　©2016　　ART: MARY FLEENER

SO EAGER IS EVERYONE TO STRIP AWAY ALL WINTER ATTIRE and SHOW OFF THEIR NEW CHESTS, NEW TATTOOS, TIGHT PACKAGES, and FIRM BUTTS THAT WHAT OFTEN GETS FORGOTTEN IN THE PRE-SPRING GROOMING PROCESS ARE FEET, ONCE SHOES and SOCKS ARE REPLACED BY FLIP FLOPS.

IF YOU'VE EVER WONDERED IF EXTRA-TERRESTRIAL LIFE EXISTS, LOOK NO FURTHER THAN EVERY 5th PERSON'S FEET. SOME RESEMBLE LOST PARTS OF RIDLEY SCOTT'S **"ALIEN".**

IT'S ENOUGH FOR ME TO HALF EXPECT SIGOURNEY WEAVER TO COME BARRELING AROUND THE CORNER TO BLAST THEM OFF.

FOR OTHERS, FEET CAN ACT AS STAND-INS FOR J.R.R. TOLKIEN'S HOBBITS OR COULD BE USED AS KLINGON FOREHEADS.

"PERHAPS TODAY IS A GOOD DAY TO DIE."*

IN OTHER WORDS, SOME PEOPLE'S FEET ARE THE CLOSEST THAT REALITY GETS TO SCIENCE FICTION.

LOOK, I FULLY UNDERSTAND THAT YOU CAN ONLY WORK WITH WHAT YOU'RE BORN WITH AND IT'S HARD ENOUGH KEEPING UP WITH UNREALISTIC SOCIETAL PRESSURES and MENTALLY CRIPPLING BODY ISSUES ETC., ETC...

98 lb
44 4452 kg

BUT THEN WHY IS IT THAT THE PEOPLE WHO NEED A PEDICURE THE MOST ARE THE ONES FLAUNTING THEIR GHASTLY HOOVES?

AND THE SOLUTION IS SO SIMPLE, TOO! IF YOU MUST INSIST ON KEEPING YOUR TOENAILS AT A GLORIOUS 3CM LENGTH ACCOMPANIED BY CORNS, FUNGUS, CALLUSES, BUNIONS, INGROWN TOENAILS and OVERGROWN TOE HAIR, COULD YOU PLEASE WRAP A SOCK AROUND YOUR EYESORES OUT OF CONSIDERATION OF PEOPLE LIKE ME WHO ALMOST UPCHUCK OUR LAST MEAL UPON FIRST SIGHT OF YOUR CREEPY PEDS?

* STAR TREK-DEEP SPACE 9... SEASON 4, EPISODE 1

WITH 8-10 THOUSAND STEPS TAKEN ON AN AVERAGE EVERY DAY, THE TOTAL DAILY FORCE EQUALING SEVERAL HUNDRED TONS, and 250,000 SWEAT GLANDS LOCATED ON EACH FOOT PAIR, IT'S ONLY NATURAL THAT ONE'S FEET TAKE SUCH A BEATING...

...THEY'LL EVENTUALLY RESEMBLE WHAT TREE TRUNKS LOOK LIKE AFTER BEING RUN THROUGH A WOOD CHIPPER OR SCHNITZELS AFTER BEING RELENTLESSLY HAMMERED BY MEAT TENDERIZERS.

I'M NOT ABOVE SCRUTINY MYSELF. IN FACT, I'M MY OWN TOUGHEST CRITIC. REST ASSURED, ANY TIME THAT WAS SPENT BY ME AT A BEACH WAS DONE WITH SOCKS AND SHOES.

BOIiiNNG!

TORONTO STAR

BEFORE ANY MORE EYEBROWS ARE RAISED, I'M NOT EXACTLY A FOOT FETISHIST, ALTHO WOMEN IN VERY REVEALING OPEN TOE HIGH HEELS WILL NEVER FAIL TO HOOK MY ATTENTION.

THINK I SOUND TOO FINICKY and DAINTY? WELL GUESS WHAT— I ALSO BELIEVE THAT MORNING BREATH SHOULD BE EXTERMINATED WITH (gasp) TOOTHPASTE and FECES BE IMMEDIATELY WIPED AWAY CLEAN WITH 3-PLY TOILET PAPER.

THERE'S NO NEED TO PUT THE WORD "HIGH" IN FRONT OF THE WORD "MAINTENANCE" WHEN IT COMES TO HOW I VIEW FOOT UPKEEP. JUST CLEAN YOUR FEET BEFORE YOU DECIDE TO SHOW THEM TO THE WORLD IN A PAIR OF SANDALS, **DAMMIT!**

SUPER WASH

DESPITE WHAT YOU MIGHT THINK, THERE'S A GOOD CHANCE YOU HAVE FEET ONLY A MOTHER COULD LOVE.

END

IT'S ONLY ROCK 'N' ROLL BUT I LIKE CHINESE FOOD

On August 16, 2002, we opened up for The Rolling Stones at the Palais Royale in our hometown of Toronto, Ontario, Canada. We got the gig at the tail end of a grinding, demoralizing Canadian tour. Loading into the club exhausted from sleep deprivation didn't quell the excitement we felt to be playing with The World's Greatest Rock 'n' Roll band. We played a good set, but everyone in the club, including the three of us on stage, just wanted to see The Stones. I made a mention of this point during our set and that seemed to gain us some sympathy from the crowd, who courteously endured us with only the slightest hint of enthusiasm.

There were a lot of life lessons to be learned from this show.

If you persevere in the music business you will eventually get to your destination; the only catch is the journey to the destination takes so long that by the time you make it there your priorities have already shifted, if not completely changed. Chasing dreams is like dealing with the devil— he can promise you a world tour, but he won't tell you that it'll be in punk rock squats all over the world filled with cockroaches and vegan food. He can promise you groupies, except they'll have cold sores and body odor. He can promise you a million people will hear your album, except that it'll be for free online and no one will like it. If there's one guarantee it's that the smell of success smells like dirty feet.

Sometimes, however, the stars align, pigs start to fly and something good happens. Like the night our band opened for The Rolling Stones.

For the rest of my life, if I never book another show, if I get fired from McDonald's, if I'm suddenly hated by my friends and family, or if I lose everything, no one will be able to take away the fact that I got to open for The Rolling Stones. When the Stones finally hang it up and someone decides to catalogue every one of their shows, there will be an entry in a ledger with our name on it. It was a magical night with The Stones in fine form playing some of my favourite songs like "Hot Stuff," "Happy" and "Can't You Hear Me Knocking," and me, on my fourth wind, taking it all in. At that moment I thought I'd peaked. Little did I know the night was only just beginning . . .

Knowing we were in the presence of the self-proclaimed (and generally accepted) Greatest Rock 'n' Roll Band In The World, one would assume the rest of the night was spent in Dionysian orgiastic delights. Indeed, this is true, but maybe not the way you might think. You see, one of the greatest pleasures to an on-the-road musician if you tour long and hard enough, is a good meal. The word "meal" isn't sexual innuendo for oral sex either. I actually mean food. It can sometimes (on the rare occasion) supersede an orgasm. Not to be crude, but there have been times on tour when I have had a woman gloriously nude in front of me but all I could think about was how I would love an order of some chicken souvlaki with some tzatziki sauce right then. It might sound hard to believe, but it's in those moments you really start to realize what's truly important in life. For me, apparently, it's food.

So it was after we had just played with the greatest rock band of all time in the history of mankind that our entourage piled back into our van and headed over to an amazing Chinese restaurant in town called New Ho King. The name always gets a few snickers because it's got the word "Ho" in it and we all figured it was entirely appropriate given that we had just played with the band that pretty much cemented the term when they wrote the song "Star Star" a.k.a. "Starfucker."

It took no time at all to place our orders since it was unusually quiet for a Friday night. Our sleep-deprived hunger was satiated almost at first bite by an almost non-stop stream of tasty platters served from their hulking menu. We threw caution to the wind and no expense was spared as platter after platter adorned our table. We definitely gave the kitchen a reason to stave off any cigarette breaks, and in the process capped off a once-in-a-lifetime night where we got both what we wanted, and what we needed.

For historical purposes, I present to you our order on that memorable night of delicious Chinese food . . . and rock 'n' roll:

Appetizers

- 201   Crispy Spring Roll $1.50 each (4 orders)
- 203   Vegetarian Egg Roll $1.25 each (4 orders)
- 206   Deep Fried Won-Ton with Sweet and Sour Sauce $3.50
- 207   Deep Fried Chicken Wings $5.50 (2 orders)

Soups

- 106   Hot and Sour Soup Large $13

Vegetable And Tofu

- 304   Mixed Vegetable Stir Fry In A Szechuan Spicy $8.50
- 314   Tofu In Oyster Sauce $7.50

Seafood

- 405   Cod With Black Bean Sauce $12.50
- 409   Seafood Feast Of Shrimps Scallops Calamari In Phoenix Nest $13.95
- 425   Shrimps With Garlic Sauce $11.95
- 430   Sauteed Calamari With Vegetable $8.95

Poultry

- 501   Ho King Special Sizzling Chicken In Hot Pot (white meat without bone) $10.95
- 506   General Tso Chicken $9.50
- 526   Orange Duck $12.95

Pork & Beef

- 611   Spicy Crispy Shredded Beef $9.95
- 634   Beef Stir Fry With Baby Bok Choi $11.50

Platter & Hot Pot

    703   Shrimp & Eggplant w/Spicy Garlic Sauce Hot Pot $10.95

    704   Braised Beef Brisket In Hot Pot $8.95

    711   Sliced Chicken w/Satay Sauce Sizzling Platter $9.95

Noodle/Rice/Chop Suey

    803   Beef With Vegetable Chow Mein $7.95

    811   Rice Noodle With Beef And Vegetable $7.95

    1007 BBQ Pork Fried Rice 6.95

    1009 Vegetable Fried Rice 6.95

    1011 Steamed Rice $1.50 (6 orders)

* I'm not gonna bother with the drink order. Let's just say it was humongous and stop there.

Here's The Rolling Stones' setlist for August 16, 2002 at Palais Royale:

"It's Only Rock 'n' roll (But I Like It)"

"Sad Sad Sad"

"If You Can't Rock Me"

"Stray Cat Blues"

"Hot Stuff"

"Don't Stop"

"Honky Tonk Women"

"Torn And Frayed"

"Wild Horses"

"Happy"

"I Can't Turn You Loose"

"Heart Of Stone"

"Can't You Hear Me Knockin'"

"Jumpin' Jack Flash"

"Brown Sugar"

A version of this piece was originally published in the September 2011 issue of Close-Up Magazine

THOUGHTS ON THE VINYL RESURGENCE

As our access to all music has gotten easier, I've quietly watched people valiantly sticking with the vinyl medium despite record store closures and the unstoppable advancement toward the digital age. While it's commendable saving an aging format in the face of tempting convenience, I can't help but note the difference in how I consumed vinyl and how others regard it today.

The introduction of compact discs in the mid-'80s created a boom period for the music industry when they successfully convinced people to rebuy what they already owned.

It was also a boom period in another sense for people like me: people burdened by an insatiable thirst to hear as much music as possible, but impeded by budgetary restraints. Since I couldn't afford the hefty $19.99 price tag that the record industry asked per compact disc release, it was most fortuitous that everyone who could afford it decided to unload their vinyl collections onto used record stores at a tenth of the price. That's when I'd swoop in and, for $20 bucks, walk out of the used record store with three or four albums under my arm. Gradually, as time went on, I was able to amass quite a substantial collection of music for a quarter of the price others were paying.

I've always noticed that there were basically two kinds of music consumers: 1) people who bought records because they needed to hear the music, and 2) people who bought records because it looked cool, especially next to their chesterfield, buffet or armoire. The first group would take their music grounded up through an AM stereo on tiny first-generation Walkman speakers, anything just to be able to hear the music. While the second group wouldn't be caught dead with anything less than a top-of-the-line stereo system.

I've also noticed the amusing inverted correlation between one's record collection and their personal stereo setup. More times than not, the higher quality the stereo system, the slimmer the collection of records/CDs a person has to play. The goal for me has never been to listen to music on the best "googlephonic stereo" with "moon rock needle," but simply to hear as much music as humanly possible before I go deaf.

I've heard the argument that the vinyl revival is the collective urge to return to the "organic" and to get back to what's "real." Vinyl records are made up of polyvinyl chloride which is the third most used plastic in the world. That doesn't sound too "organic" to me. If that isn't enough, the damn things get shrink-wrapped with, you guessed it, more plastic. It's like keeping an unpeeled banana in a ziplock bag.

Buying records was all part of a routine that, for most record collectors, became the most important part of their life after breathing and food. There was usually a specific day of the week or month that you'd hit up certain stores. It was accompanied with the anticipatory trip to said store, increased heartbeat upon entrance, explosive peak when the sought-after items were purchased, followed by the afterglow during a post-shopping bite to eat.

OK, I admit it, I still buy vinyl like some relapsing lush (I've bought three records this week already) but my issue with this recent fetishizing of vinyl has more to do with how it's treated and viewed than purchased. Vinyl records aren't pieces of furniture to be hung on walls as hipster barometers. Minus the odd collectible exception, vinyl should be scuffed, marked, worn out, scratched and (gasp) spun! If you can find a used, scratchy copy of The Beatles' *Abbey Road* for $5, it'll contain more character and charm than your freshly pressed $32 version sold at Urban Outfitters.

And don't feel bad if you haven't bought your cutting edge, ultra-modern record player yet. Unless you're an über-audiophile, what does it matter how the music is heard so long as it's heard? I've been listening to music my whole life, spent many a day in top recording studios and I still can't tell the difference between an MP3 file and a vinyl track. Maybe I've already gone deaf. Or maybe I find audiophile posturing burdensome.

On the bright side, with vinyl collecting taking off again, people are now starting to unload their CD collections and I'm waving them over with stars in my eyes the same way one waves over strippers with $5 bills.

When it comes down to it, I don't care how you wrap up the music, just as long as there's music for me to buy.

A version of this piece originally appeared May 2, 2013 on the Huffington Post *website*

THE DAY I MET JOHNNY CASH (AND SOLD HIM A NIRVANA RECORD)

WHEN WILLIE NELSON AND KRIS KRISTOFFERSON PERFORMED "THE HIGHWAYMAN" THE SIGNATURE SONG OF THEIR COUNTRY SUPERGROUP THE HIGHWAYMEN, ON THE GRAMMYS

LAST WEEK, it CONJURED UP THE ONE LONE MEMORY I HAVE OF THE BAND.

WHEN I MET THEIR FELLOW HIGHWAYMAN JOHNNY CASH...

Hi.

...AND SOLD HIM A NIRVANA RECORD.

I WAS WORKING AT MUSIC WORLD AT THE EATON CENTRE IN TORONTO BACK IN 1995.

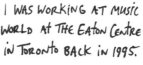

THE HIGHWAYMEN WERE IN TOWN SUPPORTING THEIR "THE ROAD GOES ON FOREVER" ALBUM IF MEMORY SERVES ME CORRECTLY.

ADMITTEDLY, I'VE NEVER BEEN A COUNTRY MUSIC FAN ALTHOUGH I CAN SAY I DO OWN MORE THAN A FEW WILLIE NELSON & JOHNNY CASH RECORDS. THEY ABOVE ANYONE ELSE IN COUNTRY MUSIC SEEMED TO EMBRACE

A BIT OF THE OLD ROCKNROLL SPIRIT THAT MADE IT EASIER FOR ME TO RELATE!

SO IMAGINE MY SURPRISE WHEN I SAW JOHNNY CASH CASUALLY STROLL BY THE STORE WITH HIS WIFE JUNE CARTER AS I STOOD MY POST LIKE A RETAIL ZOMBIE GREETER.

I TORE OUT OF THE STORE LIKE EITHER SOMEONE HAD STOLEN A BOX OF OFFSPRING CD'S OR THAT I HAD FINALLY COME TO MY SENSES AND QUIT THAT JOB.

I CAUGHT up to the couple in front of SHOPPERS DRUG MART; instead of identifying myself as a fan, engaging in small talk like a non-crazy person, I immediately started to list off all the albums I owned by Him— an albeit measely list, but impressive enough

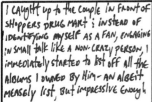

to HAVE him look at this kid dressed in HIS best Lollapalooza-come-lately uniform and ask, "Do you WORK THERE?" pointing to the MUSIC WORLD SIGN BOARD.

I NODDED A YES. Both him and CARTER exchanged what seemed to be commiserative glances. I think Johnny CASH thought I worked on commission and was trying to woo Him with A PERSONAL SALES PITCH.

um... NO. But How CAN you NOT LOVE Him FOR thinking it?

I'LL NEVER FORGET THE motherly LOOK JUNE CARTER GAVE ME WHEN SHE SAID TO CASH,

"I'LL GO HERE AND WAIT."

HERE MEANING "THE NATURE COMPANY" ACROSS the MALL, A NOW DEFUNCT RETAIL CHAIN that SOLD scientific trinkets AND NOVELTY items, while CASH went "RECORD SHOPPING" with this

STRANGE KID-FAN HE thought HE WAS KINDHEARTEDLY helping out.

MAYBE they BOTH thought the SELF-titled AMERICAN RECORDING with RICK RUBIN HE HAD just RELEASED the YEAR BEFORE WAS HAVING its effect on the ALTERNATIVE NATION. But to BE HONEST, I HADN'T EVEN HEARD the ALBUM yet.

THE look on my MANAGER Tom's FACE will be FOREVER BURNED in MY MIND when little old ME walked BACK into the store with the ONE AND ONLY JOHNNY CASH in tow.

WHAT CASH ASKED ME NEXT BLEW MY MIND. "HAVE you HEARD of NIRVANA? i'm going to BE DOING A song with them for A WILLIE NELSON tribute ALBUM AND I WANT to know what they sound like."

Yup, it was truly Johnny Cash, and the Willie Nelson song he spoke about ended up being "Time of the Preacher," done with Nirvana's Krist Novaselic

For the Twisted Willie tribute record

Eight years later I found myself on the road doing interviews for our band in a hotel room somewhere

All I can remember was a journalist from a guitar magazine telling me that Johnny Cash had just died and asking if I had any thoughts on the matter.

I told her this story and got the feeling she didn't believe me.

I didn't blame her. Why would anyone? Even before his passing, Cash had been deified to the point where an innocuous story about him such as this would seem absurd.

Hmmm...

Old rugged cross...

Despite there being no majestic entrance, no quotable proverb, no memorable exit, only a guy buying a compact disc, the whole story is true.

My greatest rocknroll moment is when I met "The Man In Black" (wearing a casual white fall jacket) at the mall.

Incredible True Tale
by Danko Jones
Barely passable artwork
by Valient Himself
3/16

A version of this piece originally appeared Feb 4th, 2014 on the Huffington Post website.

MULE WAS A ROCK BAND IN THE '90s

A mule is a mix between a donkey and a horse. Mules tend to be more intelligent than both donkeys and horses. Mixed breeds, in whatever gene pool, tend to fare better due to heterosis. One need look no further than people like Barack Obama, Bob Marley, Eddie Van Halen, Bruce Lee, Johnny Damon, Tiger Woods, Kirk Hammett and yours truly. Simply put, we rock and so did Quarterstick Recording Artists, Mule.

Born out of the ashes of Wig and sequestering the rhythm section of The Laughing Hyenas, Mule unchained their self-titled debut album in 1993 and followed up with *If I Don't Six* the year after. Living up to the band's name, the albums were filled with a mix of genres: from down-home country to crushing post-hardcore, but mostly something in between. Mule were hard to label, but easily identifiable, mostly due to singer/guitarist P.W. Long's southern-twanged, almost-indiscernible helium voice with analogous guitar and Michigan roots in hand. Throughout it all, Kevin Munro and Jim Kimball (later of Jesus Lizard fame) held down the rhythm section with the steadfastness of sturdy pack animals.

The debut Mule record is to alt-country (Wilco, Cracker, Neko Case) what Daniel Carver is to race relations, and what Jenna Jameson is to a convent. Country-tinged rock still has the ability to conjure up images of pastoral country life. It's just that Mule's version takes place in some backwoods trailer park and all characters involved are like Billy Bob

Thornton in *Sling Blade*. "Fucked" is the word I usually use, multiple times, to describe these rogue slabs of vinyl. You know these are songs from the wrong side of the tracks with titles like "What Every White Nigger Knows" and "I'm Hell."

I prefer the second half of the self-titled record, starting with the George "Shortbuckle" Roark's 1928 ditty, "Now I Truly Understand," covered acoustically by Long and followed by album highlights "Mama's Reason To Cry" (a title I ripped off for a lyric in our song "Samuel Sin" years later) and "Lucky." They're both crushing rockers that sound like Jesus Lizard having a baby in a barn.

If I Don't Six came after a year of heavy touring. Mule's tone altered slightly with Jim Kimball replacing Jake Wilson and the band a little weary from all the roadwork. Aside from the sound of a woman climaxing à la Black Flag's "Slip It In" on the album's opening cut "Hayride," most uptempo parts were wiped away in favour of a sullen, plodding approach. Tracks like "Nowhere's Back," "Piano" and "A Hundred Years" (the latter grafted into a song from P.W.'s post-Mule project "Reelfoot" under the title, "Aw Bruiser") exuded exhaustion. Even rockers like "X & 29" and my favourite cut, "Obion," eventually gave in to a great sense of tiredness.

Unfortunately, these records were met with a largely apathetic audience. The few early adopters like myself may sing the praises of this backwater rock, and magazines like *Spin* might do things like list Mule's self-titled debut as one of the best albums you never heard in 1993. But most still haven't heard Mule. With the universal appeal of alt-country, punkabilly, cowpunk, or whatever you want to call it nowadays, I still don't get why Mule didn't fare better. Why do I always back these half-asses?

A version of this piece was originally published in the July 2009 issue of Rock Star *magazine*

HELLO & THE JESUS LIZARD

I love The Jesus Lizard. Have you heard them? No, not heard *of* them, I mean actually sat down and *listened* to them. The chances of anyone saying "Yes" these days is growing smaller and smaller. Not because fans of the J.L. are dying off, but because most people are forgetting who the hell they were. After all, The Jesus Lizard did anything but live under the rug while they were around. Hell, they even made it onto a Lollapalooza line-up one year.

During the 1990s grunge/alternative zeitgeist, there existed something of an adjacent noise rock scene. While the rest of the world were appointing themselves the Alternative Nation, snapping their fingers to radio rock, it was a virtual feeding frenzy for the rest of us with bands like Cop Shoot Cop, Helmet, Tad, Unsane, Melvins, Killdozer, Distorted Pony, Johnboy, Painteens, The Cows, Wool, Mule, Nation Of Ulysses and, of course, The Jesus Lizard. Sadly, none of these bands would go on to much mass success, trampled on by alternative radio gatekeepers bent on shuffling in their versions of cute and safe "alternative" music. So if I can do my little bit to turn some people onto the amazing four-piece that slipped through the cracks then read on.

Let's put it this way, there was a time when the only band I lived for was The Jesus Lizard. I had sworn off the merits of Led Zeppelin and Slayer. Nothing seemed to be as hard as the J.L. Of course, just like every true punk rocker, once the safety pin sheen has dulled and the hair just doesn't spike up the way it used to, we all go crawling back to the used record store where we sold all our Zeppelin records and buy them back. But the appeal of The Jesus Lizard was simple. It wasn't the devil incarnate but rather an insane asylum come to life. I mean, what's scarier? Blackie Lawless eating a very rare-looking plastic steak sandwich or Hannibal Lecter?

No matter how many factoids are thrown at you to back up the claim of "world's greatest," "most underrated," or "best of," the truth is if you've never heard them you still wouldn't know jackshit as to what a band sounded like. I know it's hard to go on praising music in print without a soundbite to back you up but I'm gonna try. But how? I know I could probably give the whole *Behind The Music* biography, complete with discography, but I don't want this article to be used as makeshift toilet paper. And it still wouldn't describe The Jesus Lizard sound—a sound that comes very close to drilling a hole in your skull, prying open your brain, laying it out on the cutting board like a slab of meat and pounding away on the damaged flesh that was once a functioning brain. But, can you *hear* that?

I could give you descriptions on each member's musical prowess, how each member is a master on their respective instrument, but it wouldn't come close to seeing the quartet live, which is akin to witnessing the crucifixion of Jesus Christ. It's a surreal scene where all four morph into a hammer, driving the nails in deeper and deeper, speeding up or slowing down, getting harder or softer depending on each's daily dosage of crazy pills. Lush chords and ascending notes are played like an alarm clock with fingers, tugging the listener's pants off. But, can you *see* that?

Sure, I can reference a variety of similar-sounding bands like The Birthday Party, Gang Of Four and The Stooges, but that would just confuse things even further. You still wouldn't know that every album is a fantastic trip into the world of the absurd; a David Lynch movie going through withdrawal symptoms; a world where the women are voluptuous and mysterious while the men have Down's Syndrome. But, is that getting clearer?

OK, I know everything about the band is still about as vague as a political promise. I'm just guilty of wanting to watch tongues wag again for a band who, compared to other's popularity, remained largely a well-kept secret. Never easy to digest, The Jesus Lizard demanded the ear of the listener, which if you were apt to do so would be rewarded over and over again. Their songs were direct messages from the damned and the straight-jacketed. But their influence on the future of music remains to be seen. Maybe they'll become a band like The Stooges, whose influence took people decades to realize, but I highly doubt it. These days music is opting for flash over substance, something that, to The Jesus Lizard, would have been the most insane thing of all.

A version of this piece was originally published in the July 2005 issue of Mute *magazine*

I HATE TOMATOES

Since McDonald's fast-food restaurants were brought to their knees by Morgan Spurlock's *Supersize Me* documentary, patronage has dropped quite considerably. Despite people's growing aversion to the Golden Arches, the collective craving for a hamburger hasn't diminished, though. What's helped satiate the ground beef patty itch is the recent trend of the gourmet burger.

Even though they're three to four times more expensive than their Mickey D counterparts, most of these burgers surpass it in taste by six to eight times. For naysayers, liken it to the day you wiped your ass on three-ply toilet paper for the first time after a lifetime of using crumbling dollar store one-ply sheets and maybe then you can start to understand the difference. Remember also the day you tried going back to said one-ply paper and sadly realized you couldn't. The same can be said of the day you try your first perfectly made gourmet burger.

As the hamburger becomes a more accepted item on dinner menus, the compulsion to have the "best hamburger in town" will slowly become a mark of esteem rather than a blemish to the fine dining restaurant. In Toronto, we're seeing a hamburger renaissance where patrons are willing to wait in the blistering cold and/or fork over costly sums in order to bridge that gap between plebeian palate and refined urbanity. Raised eyebrows be damned for I am one of these people.

Recently, I visited Marben, a fine-dining restaurant in downtown Toronto that, no matter how succulent the rest of the menu is, gets

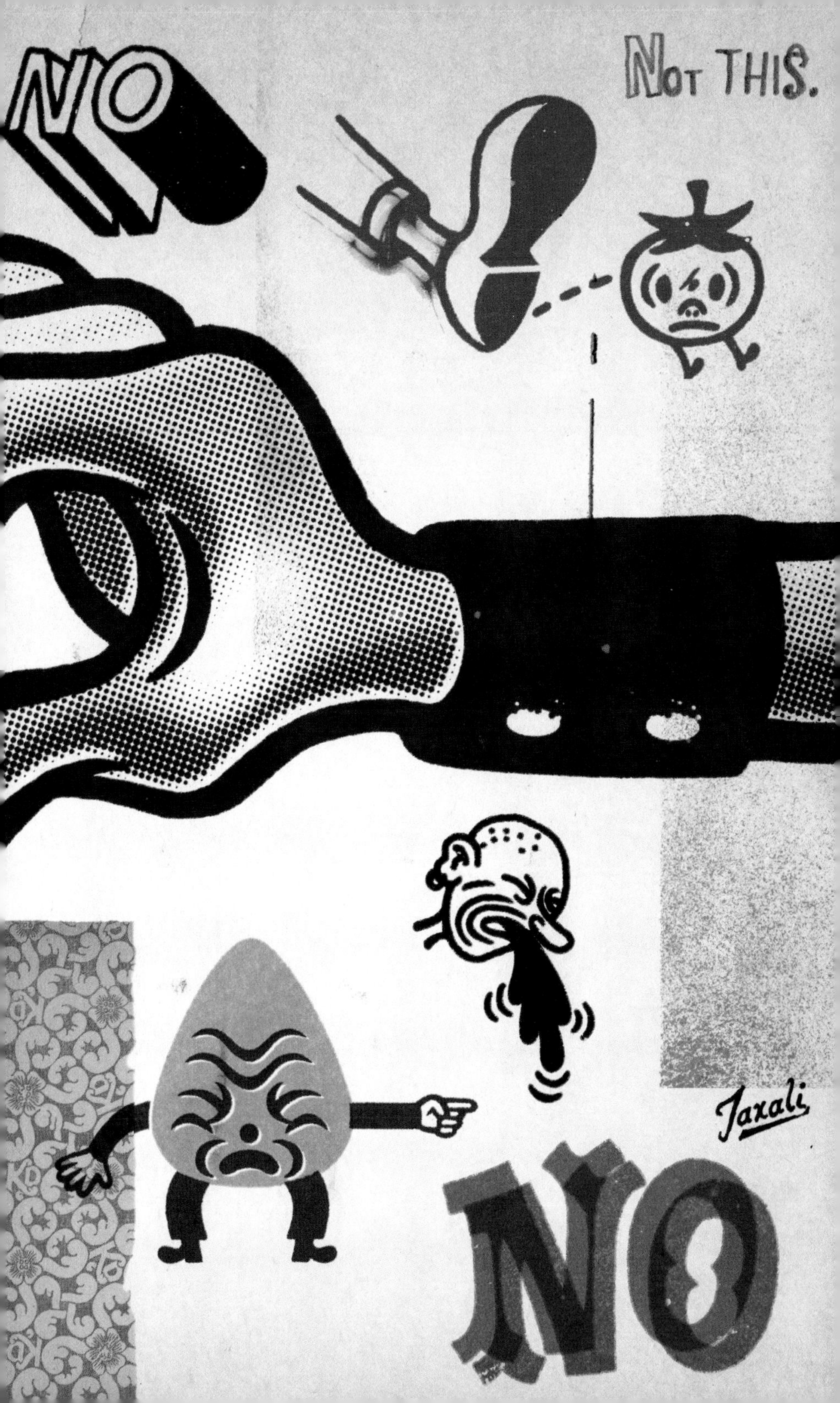

NO
NOT THIS.
Taxali
NO

introduced with a "you gotta try their burger." "John's Burger," as it's plainly named, is deliberately presented like every other burger you'd order at a greasy joint. Except that it will make the Top Ten list of best hamburgers you've ever eaten in your life.

If you haven't eaten food in the last hour or so, its description alone may get you frothing at the mouth—braised short ribs shredded and then mixed inside red angus meat from local Dingo Farms, all topped with aged cheddar and a Branston pickle spread. Describing it without using F words doesn't do it justice.

Yet, whether it's as sophisticated John's Burger or as common as the Big Mac, there's one thing they both have in common that has arguably put them a cut above the rest—no tomatoes.

I dislike tomatoes on hamburgers. Actually, I *hate* tomatoes on hamburgers. Don't get me wrong, tomatoes are fantastic on BLTs, topping salads, in tomato sauce, or with mozzarella. However, hamburgers are no place for tomatoes. Tomatoes, usually cut cold and placed chilled on top of a steaming hot beef patty, make for the most imperfect coupling in food preparation. It's like serving hot chocolate with ice cubes. Even the revolting "Hawaiian Pizza," with its pineapple topping, doesn't come close to this edible aberration. Does the proliferation of the "tomato-as-hamburger-topping" stem from a general hankering for the vegetable-like fruit? Or is it just an unconscious reflex after years of indoctrination?

For some reason there's a generally accepted selection of hamburger toppings that are automatically found on a burger and rarely with customer consultation—lettuce, mustard, ketchup and tomatoes. Even cheese, despite it being proven over and over again to increase the flavour of a hamburger from bland to scrumptious, is left to the customer to choose before ordering. While onions, due to societal concerns over one's breath, are cautiously ordered after the fact.

Whether it's hard as a rock or soft as a jellyfish, the consistency of a tomato can never compliment a hamburger. When cut crisp, its hardness ends up competing with the patty to unpalatable degrees, while when cut a tad overripe it will inevitably sog up the bun, turning an otherwise delicious meal into a wet ball.

If people think they're offsetting their risk of heart disease, high blood pressure and diabetes when eating greasy hamburgers by stuffing them with the healthy goodness of tomatoes then they're in for one rude awakening. Hell, you can put crushed multivitamins in place of chocolate sprinkles on your vanilla ice cream, but you're still gonna gain weight.

What's weirder still is that ketchup, in its essence, is made out of tomatoes, thus already bestowing the burger with tomato flavour. Why, after adding a subtle and beloved tomato-like paste, would you add real tomatoes? It's like drinking orange flavoured Kool-Aid after eating an orange.

I'm well aware that there are bigger problems in the world, but my contempt for tomatoes in hamburgers isn't a problem; it's a minor annoyance. Minor annoyances can be easily overlooked but not easily forgotten. Sometimes minor annoyances simmer quietly for years and most of the time remain left unresolved. Tomatoes on hamburgers is on a list that also includes people who stand in doorways, people who answer a text with an email or vice versa, people who make left turns over yellow lines, people who deliberately sprinkle their speech with ebonics to sound hip, negative online comments with spelling mistakes . . .

But tomatoes on hamburgers is the one annoyance that, if not dealt with first-hand, will end up sloshing around in your mouth.

A version of this piece originally appeared Feb. 23, 2013 on the Huffington Post *website. Illustration by Gary Taxali*

NEIL PEART VS MIKE BOSSY

Growing up in Canada, most boys tend to fall under at least one of two categories: a) Hockey fans, or b) Rush fans. It just comes with the citizenship kit. I definitely fall under the latter. Being that I play in a band for a living may have something to do with it; the fact that the house I grew up in is in Rush's *Subdivisions* video might have something to do with it, too. There's just something about the band that evokes automatic fandom if you're born above the 49th parallel. Maybe it's the musicianship mixed with their artistry that mirrors the rigorism and resourcefulness that Canadians navigating the country's harsh climates identify with easily. Or maybe it's just 'cause they rock.

When it comes to sports, I tendered my resignation as a hockey fan years ago. As much as I am perennially the Maple Leafs when it comes to playing video games, these days I only learn who won the Stanley Cup long after the playoffs are over. Like a lot of Canadian kids, I used to live and breathe hockey. I used to watch *Hockey Night In Canada* every Saturday night and collecting hockey cards took up most of my childhood allowance. So what exactly is it that made me fall out with the game that I loved so much as a kid?

Part of it was due to overprotective parents. Although I learned how to ice skate at a very early age, I was never allowed to play organized minor hockey. With the recent discussions on the link between hockey and concussions, maybe my mom was right to make me sit out hockey and take up soccer instead. I still wish that whenever I laced up my skates I would've been holding a stick, though.

But my mom's embargo on playing hockey only fuelled my love for the game. Not being allowed to do something just makes anyone thirst for it even more. As much as I wanted my beloved Leafs to win something, anything, I slowly got wooed over to the other side and, to my own surprise, became a New York Islanders fan. The Islanders created a dynasty in the 1980s and their line-up read like an all-star hockey game on its own—Clark Gillies, Butch Goring, Billy Smith, Bryan Trottier, Bob Nystrom and my favourite hockey player, Mike Bossy.

I loved Mike Bossy. I loved him so much that my mom wrote into the Canadian show, *Thrill Of A Lifetime*, probably out of guilt for not letting me actually play hockey, and told them so.

Thrill Of A Lifetime was a popular show that ran for six seasons on the CTV network that invited viewers to write in and tell them their dreams, their "thrill of a lifetime," so to speak. If picked, the show would do their best to make that person's "thrill" happen. Playmate of the year Shannon Tweed had her dream fulfilled when she was granted an audition with *Playboy* magazine and we all know how that turned out. Whether it was wanting to fly a jet fighter, swim with dolphins, or appearing as an extra on a television show, *Thrill Of A Lifetime* would make it happen.

The show's producers responded to my mom's letter in turn by contacting us, interviewing me and asking what I'd do with Mike Bossy if I got the chance to hang out with him for a day. Me, being a dumb kid, said something to the effect of "Go to a movie?" I immediately received my first "Don't call us, we'll call you." It never dawned on me that, from a television show's standpoint, watching people watching movies was boring as fuck. What I should've said was "PLAY HOCKEY WITH MIKE BOSSY."

When I watched another person get to PLAY HOCKEY with Mike Bossy the following season (season 2, episode 8) I was devastated. I was devastated to the point that even to this day I change the subject if his name is brought up in conversation, or change the channel if he just happens to be on television. I also never watched the show again.

From that point, my interest in hockey declined to the point of irrelevance in my life.

On the other hand, my fandom for Rush has only increased. I became aware of them around the time they released *Signals*. But, believe it or not, it was *Grace Under Pressure* that got me into the band and I worked my way backwards through their discography after that. Sure, they can be an acquired taste, but if you stay the course they will return your effort tenfold.

Touring around the globe, you quickly realize that Rush are so synonymous with Canada that when people find out we're Canadian it only takes five minutes before they start giving us their best "Tom Sawyer" or "Closer To The Heart" air guitar impression. Rush are good ambassadors for our country—lionized yet gracious, cultivated yet robust.

Rush drummer Neil Peart has even become an author in recent years and reading some of his books inspired me to send him a handwritten fan letter in 2004. After years of seeing behind the velvet curtain and turning my ever-growing jadedness into a fine pointy lance, I'm still not above writing fan letters. OK fine, I admit I was able to circumvent Canada Post and deliver it directly to a certified Rush team member, but Peart is infamously known to be somewhat reclusive. I didn't expect an answer back, and being that I was a lot older now, just the writing of it was enough to make me feel good.

Still, ever the jaded hopeful, I waited for a reply.

Years passed, 2004 turned into 2005, 2005 turned into 2006, 2006 turned into 2007 . . .

Then, November 2007 I received a handwritten reply from Peart in the mail. It had taken so long that I had forgotten I even wrote the letter in the first place. My heart stopped, my pulse raced, my brow beaded.

Neil Peart had written me back!

Since then I've probably stared at Neil Peart's letter so much that it's totalled hours. I've played air drums in front of it, I've played air bass to it and I've used it to pick me up when I was down. I've even talked to it.

It took almost a lifetime, but I finally got my thrill.

Peart 1, Bossy 0

A version of this piece originally appeared May 31, 2013 on the Huffington Post *website*

R.I.P. RAVI SHANKAR

When it comes to music, my parents and I have never seen eye to eye. Let's face it, my parents and I have never seen eye to eye on most things. If they say stop, I say go. If they say white, I say black.

Over time, and through much trial and error, we have learned to construct invisible lines in the sand in order to keep each other in our lives. And even though it might be a facade that buries the issues that keep us from truly emotionally connecting again, some may say that it's better than not being in each other's lives at all. No matter how many issues we have with each other, at the end of the day, we love each other, albeit tumultuously.

I am very grateful to my parents whether they realize it or not. I'm grateful to them for instilling me with a set of morals that I use as a compass to this day. I am grateful for their love and care and their best intentions for me at all times. And I am grateful for that night they took me out, way past my bedtime when I was eight years old, to see Ravi Shankar play with Alla Rakha at the Minkler Auditorium, which used to be part of the Seneca College Newnham Campus in Willowdale, Ontario.

Did I have a clue as to who I was watching that night? Absolutely not. I do remember that I was completely un-psyched to be in the audience before the show started. I saw a few longhairs and figured it must be a rock concert of some sort, but knew my parents HATED rock music so it was confusing. I capitalize the word "hate" because nothing has changed with them to this day.

When the show started, my recollections are vague probably due to my young wandering mind and my wish of not wanting to be there. How I wonder what Shankar would've thought knowing that no matter how much the entire room, the entire world, revered his playing, there was an eight-year-old kid in the crowd just wishing he was at home playing with his *Empire Strikes Back* action figures.

My most vivid memory of watching this intimate performance, in basically a glorified college lecture hall, is watching Shankar play on the floor with his eyes closed, which I found mildly impressive, while his trusted tabla player, Alla Rakha, beat out rhythms by his side.

No matter how many great bands and great shows I've witnessed over the years, there's no show that carries the weight of this one. I guess you can say it's been all downhill since. And even though I didn't appreciate the moment while it was happening, I remember what I had seen 15 years later like a thunderbolt to my mind. My brain was being expanded and my music tastes widening. I remember sitting in my room years later kicking myself for not taking it all in properly. Even when I found out Shankar had passed away late this past Tuesday, it took me a full 10 minutes to remember that I had indeed seen him perform all those many years ago, so distant is the remembrance.

I never did see Shankar perform live again, but over the years my love for classical Indian Music has grown to the point where I even took Trichy Sankaran's world music class at York University years ago.

When my father made a home trip to New Delhi one year, I begged him to bring back as much Shankar music as he could fit in his luggage. I think the request surprised him, but he gladly obliged. Coming from a household where academia was valued above all else and seeing the quiet sting of disappointment in my parent's eyes when I chose a musical vocation, they can't deny that by exposing me to Ravi Shankar at such an early age had an effect. In a way, they were complicit in this rock 'n' roll thing I call a "job."

Pandit Ravi Shankar, Aapki Aatma Ko Shanti Mile

A version of this piece originally appeared Dec. 14, 2012 on the Huffington Post *website*

THE 30 YEARS OF BLACK SABBATH MIXTAPE

Most people, when you mention Black Sabbath, will knee-jerk into their rendition of "Iron Man" or "Sweet Leaf" on air guitar, yearn for the *Mob Rules* days with Ronnie James Dio, or wax nostalgic about Ozzy Osbourne. The only problem is that Ozzy was in the band 34 years ago! That's a lifetime into adulthood for people and some may argue that Ozzy's tenure in Sabbath truly ended a long time ago. Granted, they're finally back in the studio readying a new album, but it comes when all of them are past their prime.

With Tony Iommi recently diagnosed with lymphoma and drummer Bill Ward controversially left out of the reunion recording, some aren't even considering this new venture a true "Black Sabbath" album. But these kinds of dismissals aren't new for a band that have, for the past 30 years, been putting out records to virtually no fanfare. You see, even though Black Sabbath have existed for 43 years, most people (and when I say most I mean 95 per cent of people) only acknowledge the first 11 years of their discography—from the 1970's self-titled album through to 1981's *Mob Rules* when Dio was the band's lead singer.

In 2013 we'll be marking 30 years of Black Sabbath music that nobody even knows about. *Born Again*, the album from 1983 with Ian Gillan, marked the beginning of three decades of creative floundering, endless line-up changes and waning Sabbath crowds while Ozzy's solo stature rose. But no matter what anybody says, there are diamonds to be found in those 30 years. I've put together a mixtape of Sabbath gems from this lost period and there isn't one hint of "Paranoid" in the lot.

Here's what's on it:

"Hotline" (1983)

A sleaze riff that might've been inspired by the burgeoning L.A. glam scene being this was released in 1983. I could definitely hear Mötley Crüe recording this ditty for *Too Fast For Love*. Either way, this is a testament to Ian Gillan's voice as he elevates the sleaze to a tempered fist.

"Seventh Star" (1986)

One thing the Iommi/Dio collaborations always had was a need to make the title track the slow, doomy one on their respective albums. For *Seventh Star*, Iommi brought in ex-Deep Purple bassist/vocalist Glen Hughes, and as much as I think Hughes is a phenomenal singer, I don't think his voice was ever meant for Black Sabbath. However, here the riffs blend well with his vox.

"Lost Forever" (1987)

Why this chugger was buried on *The Eternal Idol* album is beyond me. If anything, it should've followed "The Shining" on side one. A dismal album overall, but tracks like this preserve some dignity.

"Evil Eye" (1994)

A song spun around a Sabbath riff that harkens back to past glory, only it wasn't Iommi who wrote it, but rather Eddie Van Halen. Eddie isn't credited on the *Cross Purposes* record, merely thanked, but both Tony Martin and Geoff Nicholls have confirmed that Eddie wrote and played the riff. It was only due to anticipated record label conflicts that Iommi recorded over it and both parties chose to leave its authorship a mystery.

"Sins Of The Father" (1992)
Rock fans held their collective breath when Dio signed on to rejoin Geezer and Iommi long enough to release *Dehumanizer*, but disappointment reigned when this reunion eventually ended six months later. At least we were left with songs like this one.

"Can't Get Close Enough" (1995)
As great as this song is, it would've been so much better on classic Sabbath albums like *Sabotage*, especially if Ozzy was allowed at it. Nothing to take away from Tony Martin's vocals, but it really reveals that his Sammy Hagar-meets-Ronnie James Dio-inspired vocals don't hold a candle to Ozzy Osbourne. Not by a mile.

"What's The Use" (1994)
An impressive song, but if one just closes their eyes for a minute and concentrates, it's obvious the song would've blossomed under Dio's watch. And perhaps it should have even been chosen to open *Cross Purposes* instead of it being buried as the last track. Tony Martin ends up sounding like Dio's understudy here.

"Zero The Hero" (1983)
This was the hit single off of *Born Again* and a beloved Sabbath song that often gets overlooked. Everybody knows it, but aren't quick enough to rattle it off when it comes to listing notable Sabbath tunes. I can't overlook it on this list.

"Loser Gets It All" (1995)
The last song of the last Black Sabbath album and a fitting curtain call.

"Master Of Insanity" (1992)
Maybe the reason this song sounds great, besides Dio's return to the Sabbath fold, is that the main riff is a direct ripoff of Judas Priest's "A Touch Of Evil," released just two years previous to the *Dehumanizer*

album this song is off. I'm sure it wasn't deliberate so much as it's proof of how incredible Priest's *Painkiller* album is.

"Angry Heart" (1986)

This sounds like Mark 3 Deep Purple, maybe something off of *Burn* or *Stormbringer*, but hardly reminiscent of anything the band that wrote "Symptom Of The Universe" or "Turn Up The Night" ever played. It's a nice departure, but more proof Hughes wasn't supposed to sing over Iommi riffs for too long.

"The Sabbath Stones" (1990)

A solid heavy metal song and Tony Martin lays out a great vocal. I know this article is supposed to showcase Sabbath's disregarded eras, but it's too obvious that even in their finer moments they still sound like a band heavily influenced by Sabbath. Call me silly but to me they could do no wrong.

A version of this piece was originally published in the April 2013 issue of Close-Up Magazine

The Music Festival for Heavy Music Lovers

There are two kinds of people in this world — people who listen to music and people who don't. They think they listen to music, but they really don't. These are people who listen to what's spoon-fed to them by a variety of cursory sources i.e. car radio, magazine cover, iTunes banner, billboard, movie theme song, etc. Some people will obsessively listen to one record or one band or one music genre over and over again and consider themselves music lovers. They're only music listeners in the same way someone who travels to Disneyland every summer calls themselves a world traveler.

These desultory listeners need to have this reality clarified for them because real music listeners are music lovers and they truly are a special breed. There are several tiers to this distinction. For example, when placed beside someone like Damian Abraham, singer of Fucked Up, I pale in comparison because I don't think I'd spend $1,800 on a Negative Approach single like he did. So some are more fervent than others. But at its core a real music listener has a compulsion to listen to as much "good" music as possible before one dies, regardless of genre.

To me, there are only two types of music in the world — good and bad. I like to listen to the good kind. Music is surely relative, but when one looks at the music that gets continually lauded over, be it critically or at a mainstream level, there's usually a complete dismissal of anything remotely hard or heavy. Reason being is that, to most, the brashness of heavy music is seen as vulgar and uncouth, and that's not even counting its lyrics.

I've always been stupefied by this generally accepted idea. Nobody on either side of the fence even bothers an attempt to rectify heavy music's perception as unsophisticated. Meanwhile, bands like Cult Of Luna, Shining, Sons Of Otis and dozens of others proffer servings of beautiful cacophony that are on par with any recognized and critically accepted music act.

For years I've been a very outspoken booster for all things hard and heavy while I quietly listened to music acts like The Dears, Stereolab, Broken Social Scene, Smog and Bedhead. It wasn't out of embarrassment or shame, but rather out of a futile attempt to even up what I saw as uneven attention going to softer musics. I still stand behind the notion that A Sun That Never Sets by Neurosis is just as, if not more, beautiful and rapturous as Elliot Smith's XO album, but most people haven't even heard Neurosis so it loses that debate on the ignorance vote.

There is for people like me, however, an oasis called The Roadburn Festival that represents everything that I've vaunted for years. Roadburn's a four-day annual event in Tilburg, Holland (April 18 to 21, 2013) catering to heavy music lying outside of agreed upon music boundaries. From its early beginnings as a website dedicated to stoner rock and doom in the late-'90s to evolving into an internationally attended festival of renown, Roadburn harnesses a new list of underground bands each year with little stature, but rabid followings and collectively stuffs them into the 013, a venue that can hold just over 2,000 people. Each passing year the festival sells out months in advance without fail, proving there is an audience for this music.

Unlike other esteemed festivals like Coachella, Roadburn refuses to kowtow to commercial acts, sticking to their mandate of "... creat(ing) an adventurous festival we would want to attend as music lovers," as said by co-founder and artistic director, Walter Hoeijmakers. He further reiterates, "We want Roadburn to be this festival as a tribute to the open-mindedness of the music lover."

Any sense of musical adventure would be lost if forced to crowbar triple-A acts like Red Hot Chilli Peppers or Kanye West and thankfully Roadburn knows this.

What's probably the most endearing part of the festival is their curated line-ups overseen in the past by such highly respected bands like Electric Wizard, Triptykon, Voivod and Sunn O))). It's this curating angle, as well as their clever underground band choices, that earns Roadburn the cred other more commercial festivals fail to capitalize on — the marked interest in bands as fans themselves.

Although my band is probably looked upon as too commercial by most Roadburn attendees, I'm still throwing my hat in the ring as potential curator. I love the running orders and regardless of what music I play, it doesn't stop me from listening to this music, too — music meant to push, elate, explore, bludgeon and deafen.

If I could hold Roadburn in rapture for one night it might go like this:

Moving Sidewalks (HEADLINER)
Diamanda Galas (HEADLINER)

Jandek
Zeitkratzer
(Plays Metal Machine Music)
OR
Zeitkratzer with Keiji Haino
Nifelheim
Zombi
Grand Magus
Brant Bjork & The Bros
Ben Frost
Yamantaka Eye
Church Of Misery
Shining (Norge)
Sacrifice
Gentleman's Pistols
Hirax
The Doomriders
Colin Stetson
Brothers Of The Sonic Cloth
Sons Of Otis
Burning Love
Bombass
Danava
Beaver
Evil United

A version of this piece originally appeared March 9, 2013 on the Huffington Post website. Art by Away.

CROWNING THE KING OF ROCK 'N' ROLL

"Why would anyone leave The Hellacopters now?" I said to myself, staring at a promo poster for the Backyard Babies' sophomore album, *Total 13*, hanging on the walls of the now defunct Toronto punk rock record store, Full Blast. The Backyard Babies, from Nässjö, Sweden, were a rock 'n' roll quartet who, along with The Hellacopters from Stockholm, helped ignite the Scandinavian rock revival of the 1990s. Backyard Babies guitarist Andreas Tyrone Svensson, a.k.a. Dregen, co-founded both bands and was playing in both bands until mounting schedules from either side forced him to make a decision. Ultimately, he chose to leave behind the growing fanfare and Stateside interest of The Hellacopters to build it up again with his childhood buddies in the Backyard Babies. It was definitely admirable, but as someone who was chasing the opportunity to make this rock thing more than just a hobby myself, it was baffling.

In the mid- to late-1990s garage rock was a thriving underground scene with bands like New Bomb Turks, Teengenerate, The Oblivions, The Makers, The Devil Dogs, Rocket From The Crypt, Jon Spencer Blues Explosion, The Supersuckers and The Hellacopters at the top of the heap. Of course, this scene eventually died down, but not before bands like The Hives and The White Stripes achieved overground success. When it comes to Scandinavia's contribution, what started with The Hellacopters, Gluecifer and Backyard Babies continues to thrive today with bands like

Imperial State Electric, Audrey Horne, Royal Republic, The Night Flight Orchestra, Free Fall, Bombus, Horisont, Witchcraft, Crystal Caravan and Bullet, not to mention Denmark's Volbeat, who pretty much own the rock scene in the States.

When we ended up playing with The Hellacopters for their U.S. debut at the CMJ Music Festival in 1998 on the eve of their third release *Grande Rock,* the line-up to get into the show snaked around the nightclub. Midway into their set a friend leaned over to me and yelled, "They're missing their key guy." He meant Dregen. Having only seen his picture on the back of the *Supershitty To The Max* Hellacopters album and the *Total 13* promo poster, I didn't really know what he meant, but still the question lingered, "Why would anyone leave The Hellacopters now?"

Fast forward to 2001 where we found ourselves on our first European tour playing the Malmo City Festival with none other than Backyard Babies. Now was my chance to see what was worth passing up the elusive wave of tastemaker approval and Hellacopters hype. It took me only three minutes to understand. Here I was thinking Dregen's decision to leave The Hellacopters, however commendable, was ill-advised and presumptuous, only to realize it was probably the best move he ever made. I watched with mouth agape as Backyard Babies tore through their set, churning out airtight hard rock, the kind of hard rock that makes you hum while you let it kick your ass. Each member was locked in, hair whipping to and fro, veins bulging and faces in blissful grimace. And there was Dregen, near-airborne with charisma shooting out of him like the stars one sees after getting punched in the face. He was Johnny Thunders, Iggy Pop, Angus Young, Nikki Sixx and Ace Frehley all mashed together. He was spellbinding.

A few weeks later we found ourselves sharing a tour bus with Backyard Babies across Europe supporting them while they promoted their *Making Enemies Is Good* album. We didn't know each other at all beyond having seen each other's sets, but here we were for six weeks in the closest of quarters on a stinky rock bus. What could've been the worst experience of my life turned into quite possibly the best tour we've ever done. The camaraderie established on this tour continues to this day.

Beyond the music itself, rock 'n' roll has always stood for freedom to me. Its lead characters embody this freedom in a way the music only attempts to describe. So huge are these personalities that often one name is all they need. It's understood that Elvis was king, but whether people know it or not, the title of King has long been superseded by Jimi, Keith, Ozzy, Lemmy and Iggy.

Even though it's hard to accept, as each of these figures move further away from their golden years, the inevitable search to find their heirs begins. These get tougher and tougher to spot in a world where being an individual is sold to the masses in convenient starter kits and where tattoo sleeves are as pedestrian as a new hat or a new pair of pants. It's getting hard to differentiate the genuine articles from the impersonators when everything we know and hold dear inevitably gets co-opted, gentrified and codified.

Luckily, after being able to stay above water for almost 20 years in the music biz, my bullshit detector is fit enough to wade through the thickest of posers and capable enough to discern bona fide successors from the Pacific Mall knock-offs. And now on the eve of his long-awaited debut solo album, simply titled *Dregen*, the man stands poised, ready to assume his rightful dominion. Hell, he knew this was to be his long before anyone else figured it out.

Hail, Hail Dregen, King of Rock and that slippery Roll.

A version of this piece originally appeared Sept. 10, 2013 on the Huffington Post *website*

WANT TO WIN AN AWARD? BECOME A CANADIAN MUSICIAN

It seems like everyone I know gets their furniture at Ikea. No matter whose home I visit, I end up seeing Ikea bookshelves, tables, drawers, futons, lamps, rugs, towels and pillowcases. Despite it being an inexpensive depot for novice homeowner/renters, it can get pretty damn boring. In order to separate yourself from the rest of the heap, there needs to be some distinguishing pieces of furniture. One's wallspace allows for framed photos or tasteful artwork to be hung. Side tables allow for smaller accessories like picture frames, lamps, candles, plants, statues or discerning hardcover books to be displayed. But to really set yourself apart from everyone, awards must be exhibited, be they plaques, trophies, ribbons, badges or statuettes. So how do you procure such items of distinction if you only have a modicum of talent? You join the Canadian music business.

I honestly can't tell you the exact number of distinct music award ceremonies there are in Canada because I lost count at 33; that's not even counting the award galas that honour "the arts," which end up usually distributing token prizes to music, too. Nor does it count the "reader's polls" of various monthlies, weeklies and dailies across the country.

Of course, there's the glorious Juno Awards, Canada's most prestigious music award ceremony. Nationally televised, the Junos are acclaimed enough to attract not only famed Canadians back to the homefront, but international performers as well. Past hosts have included Shania Twain, Russell Peters, Pamela Anderson and William Shatner. However, if one fails to win a Juno in one of its 44 categories or other national award ceremonies like The CASBYs (Canadian Artists Selected By You) or the INDIES (Canadian Independent Music Awards), there are many more opportunities to be decorated.

Failing the national awards, there are always regional/provincial awards. Western Canadian Music Awards for our western provinces, and East Coast Music Awards for our Maritime ones. There are also the Vancouver Island Music Awards, the Prince Edward Island Music Awards, Music Nova Scotia Awards, Music New Brunswick Awards. Looking more central there's the Félix Awards (Quebec), the Quebec Independent Music Awards and the Niagara Music Awards. However, if one is unsuccessful at bagging a provincial/regional award there are even more award shows to sustain one's chances.

Depending on what city you live in there are award shows at the municipal level like the Edmonton Music Awards, the Calgary Music Awards, the Vancouver Music Awards, the Hamilton Music Awards and the London Music Awards. If you live in Toronto, for example, and are an independent musician/band, you can be eligible for The Toronto Independent Music Awards, but failing that, one can move 40 minutes away to Mississauga and be eligible for certain categories in their "MARTY" awards. If one finds himself still coming up empty at the municipal level, there are yet even more Canadian music awards up for grabs.

An almost surefire way to receive a Canadian music award is if you specialize. Barring the national and provincial categories, country music provides the best odds to receive a music award in Canada with their own Canadian Country Music Awards, Northern Ontario Country Music Awards, Saskatchewan Country Music Association Awards, Alberta Country Music Awards, British Columbia Country Music Awards and Country Music

Association Of Ontario Awards. And if country music isn't your bag, there are the Canadian Reggae Music Awards, the Canadian Folk Music Awards, the Covenant Awards, the Polaris Music Prize and the Canadian Urban Music Awards.

If you're more of a behind-the-scenes player, working in the industry in marketing and promotion, running a music venue, working as a booking agent, promoter, record store owner or manager and still want an award, there are specialized industry shows just for you. There's the Canadian Music And Broadcast Industry Awards with categories such as "Music Journalist/Blogger Of The Year" and its 10 nominees. There's even the humorous category of "Best Major Label Of The Year." Interestingly, there are only three nominees in this category. For songwriters, there are the SOCAN Awards. For music video directors, cinematographers and editors there are the MuchMusic Video Awards and the Prism Prize. For people in radio there are the Canadian Radio Music Awards.

By now, it's quite obvious you can't throw a stone without receiving a Canadian music award. If you manage to obtain a few of them, or even one of the several "lifetime achievement" awards that are available, you might be eligible for an even further distinction—induction into a hall of fame. There's the Canadian Music Hall Of Fame, Canada's Walk Of Fame, Canadian Country Hall Of Fame, Ottawa Valley Country Music Hall Of Fame, Nova Scotia Country Music Hall Of Fame, Manitoba Country Music Association Hall Of Fame, British Columbia Country Music Hall Of Fame, Canadian Songwriters Hall Of Fame and even the Canadian Music Industry Hall Of Fame. I've most likely overlooked a half-dozen more, too.

Despite the abundant amount of music awards to be had in Canada our band has never received one.

I'm fully aware there's the loud majority that think we have no business winning any sort of award. They're probably right. Still, I have to be honest, for years this rebuff has bothered me, yearning for the acknowledgement from our peers and the approval of our seniors. But I'm a naturally superstitious person and have started to believe our slow, continual upward trajectory as a band who has played on six continents in over 30 countries over the last 17 years has something to do with the fact that we've never won a Canadian music award.

I now almost pray we're ignored by Canadian award events when they disperse their yearly nominations. Trust me, I wish I had a whole pile of them to display at home, but not at the superstitious risk of giving up what we've been able to achieve without one. Also, because I've watched almost every person I know snag one, the shine of scoring a Canadian music award is now lost. It's almost like when each kid gets a prize at a children's birthday party.

I'm more than happy to settle with paying the next batch of deserving winners the customary compliments and continuing on my way.

A version of this piece originally appeared Sept. 30, 2013 on the Huffington Post *website*

I'M TIRED OF USING THE DEVIL HORN HAND GESTURE IN PICTURES. I'VE GROWN TO HATE IT. EVERY SINGLE PERSON AND THEIR MOM USE IT NOW. AVRIL LAVIGNE AND JADA PINKETT-SMITH USE IT IN PHOTOGRAPHS. LAY PEOPLE USE IT TO LOOK TOUGH (THEY LOOK STUPID). I LOOK STUPID DOING IT AND SO DO YOU. IT'S OVERDONE. IT'S HAD ITS TIME. WE SHOULD ALL STOP DOING IT AND TRY SOMETHING NEW.

WHAT EXACTLY DO DEVIL HORNS MEAN ANYWAY? WITH THE THUMB DOWN AND THE INDEX AND PINKY FINGER UP, IT'S COMMONLY KNOWN TO BE A SIGN OF THE DEVIL. OUTWARDLY, THE GESTURE IS SUPPOSED TO REPRESENT THE DEVIL'S HORNS. CLOSER INSPECTION SHOWS THAT THERE ARE INDEED THREE SIXES THAT FORM ON ONE'S HAND. ONE SIX ON EACH SIDE OF THE HAND AND A THIRD SIX FORMED BY THE THUMB, RING AND MIDDLE FINGER DOWN. THESE THREE FINGERS FOLDED DOWN ALSO SYMBOLIZE THE DENIAL OF THE HOLY TRINITY.

ACTUALLY, THAT DOES SOUND PRETTY SCARY!

OFTEN THE GESTURE IS MISTAKENLY FLASHED WITH A THUMB STICKING OUT. LAY USERS OFTEN THINK THIS IS THE DEVIL HORN SIGN. WRONG. IN FACT, THE THUMB STICKING OUT TURNS THE MEANING ON IT'S HEAD AND BECOMES THE "ILY SIGN" OR "I LOVE YOU" WITH THE PINKY STANDING FOR "I", THE FOREFINGER AND THUMB FORMING "L" TO MEAN "LOVE" AND THE PINKY AND FOREFINGER FORMING "Y" TO MEAN "YOU". YES INDEED; IN PRACTICALLY EVERY FIFTH SHOT OF SOME BAND TRYING TO LOOK TOUGH THEY'RE ACTUALLY TELLING THE WORLD "I LOVE YOU".

I LOVE YOU! ARGHHHHH!!!

IT IS A GESTURE THAT, OVERTIME, HAS HAD CONFLICTING USES. ON ONE HAND, PEOPLE HAVE USED IT TO WARD OFF AND EXPEL EVIL. ON THE OTHER HAND, IT HAS RECENTLY COME TO REPRESENT THE VERY THING OTHERS TRY TO EXPEL. CONFUSED? NOT NEARLY AS MUCH AS I AM.

FURTHERMORE, IN THE LAST 15 TO 20 YEARS, THE ADVENT OF MTV, THE UBIQUITY OF "ENTER SANDMAN", THE OSBOURNE'S CARTOONISH REALITY SHOW AND THE GENERAL MAINSTREAM ACCEPTANCE OF HEAVY METAL, DEVIL HORNS HAVE BECOME AS CLICHED AS A CELEBRATORY HIGH-FIVE OR BLOWING OUT CANDLES ON A BIRTHDAY CAKE.

IN ROCK AND ROLL MANY PROMINENT MUSICIANS HAVE CLAIMED OWNERSHIP ON THE HORNS. GENE SIMMONS OF KISS HAS CLAIMED TO HAVE INVENTED THE GESTURE BY SIMULATING A MONSTER CLAW WHILE HOLDING HIS GUITAR PICK. RONNIE JAMES DIO CLAIMED IT WAS HIS GRANDMOTHERS WAY OF FENDING OFF EVIL SPIRITS. BUT THE FIRST EVER R'N'R USAGE THAT I KNOW OF WAS ON COVEN'S 1969 ALBUM "WITCHCRAFT DESTROYS MINDS AND REAPS SOULS" THAT DEPICTED A SATANIC CEREMONY. BUT IF YOU WANT TO GO BACK IN HISTORY, DEVIL HORN USAGE CAN BE FOUND IN LATE 14TH CENTURY ARABIC ILLUSTRATIONS OF SATAN.

I INVENTED IT!!

NO! I DID!!

IF THE DEVIL HORNS ARE TRULY MEANT TO REPRESENT EVIL AND ACT AS A THREATENING GESTURE, WHY AM I MORE SCARED TO SHAKE SOMEONE'S HAND THAN SOMEONE FLASHING ME THE HORNS WITH SAID HAND? DO YOU KNOW HOW MANY THINGS PEOPLE DO WITH THEIR HANDS WITHOUT WASHING THEM AFTERWARDS? IT'S JUST ABOUT THE SCARIEST THING KNOWN TO MAN. IN FACT, IF THERE WAS A HAND GESTURE TO SIGNIFY UNWASHED HANDS, THAT WOULD BE ENOUGH TO SCARE THE LIVING HELL OUT OF ME...

..NICE TO MEET YOU, DUDE!!

WORDS: DANKO JONES / PICTURES: BRIAN WALSBY, 2016.

A LIFETIME OF FANDOM FOR DEATH ANGEL

Death Angel are one of my all-time favourite bands. I remember seeing people around Toronto wearing their shirts, not sure of who they were and yet intuitively knowing that was *my band*, kinda like when you see someone across a crowded room and sparks fly. I went and bought their only album out at the time, 1987's *Ultra-Violence*. Metallica were epic; Slayer were evil; but this was the rawest, most obnoxious piece of metal I had ever heard up 'til then. It remains in my top 10 metal albums of all-time. Through countless listens, it has the unshakable ability to be as fresh and bone-crushing as the day I first heard it, despite them laughing at my sorry ass when I first met them when I was 16.

When you're young, dumb, awkward and shy, getting laughed at can get embedded in your psyche. A big reason a lot of kids got into heavy metal, before it got streamlined into the worldwide popular movement it is today, was due to its outsider appeal. So when Death Angel had just released their follow-up album *Frolic Through The Park* I went to the autograph session at the Record Peddler in Toronto and endured singer Mark Osegueda and drummer Andy Galeon's outburst of laughter when they took one look at me. I was probably asking for it since I was the only one in line dumb enough to show up in their school uniform, tie included.

I did feel like a dork, but Mark and Andy's open guffaw confirmed it. I meekly gathered up their signatures and replayed the event in my mind all the way home on the subway.

Regardless of their teasing, I stayed with them through thick and thin, holding a vigil through their 14 year absence, all the way to their reformation and subsequent return with 2004's *Art Of Dying*. I've cheered on every successive album like it was my own. It was easy to do when superb albums like *Act 3* got released, but still, shouldn't there be a ribbon one gets for such loyalty?

Flash forward to 2004 in Helsinki, Finland, when I walked into the lobby of the hotel we were staying at only to find out our promoter had to head immediately back to the airport to pick up Death Angel, who were staying at the same hotel. Instead of succumbing to an immediate heart attack, I opted to camp out in the lobby like some One Direction fan and awaited their arrival for almost two hours. As luck would have it, we ended up hanging out with them that night in a club across the street until 4 a.m. Still, imitating moss growing on a wall while creepily ogling the Death Angel quintet can hardly be called "hanging out." They acknowledged me with polite "heys" and head nods, perhaps as a safety precaution due to my creepy leering, but I was too busy proudly texting friends back home to notice.

Over the past nine years, that night has sprouted into genuine friendship. I have to constantly pinch myself whenever an email from one of the Death Angel guys hits my inbox and whatever I'm doing is immediately made to wait as I painstakingly craft my reply. Getting invited to sing "Bored" with them on stage for Hellfest in France back in 2008 and "Thrashers" at a recent Toronto show was the equivalent of winning an MTV Lost Weekend contest or a visit from Ed McMahon with a winning sweepstakes ticket. To say I was stoked would be a towering understatement.

In 2010, the band released their sixth and most devastating album to date, *Relentless Retribution*. It's a 12-song salvo of foaming rage rarely heard from bands half their age. It was an impressive middle finger that turned heads, dropped jaws, soiled pants and immediately vaulted them into their rightful status of respected elder statesman of the metal militia. As much as I was extremely happy for their success, I couldn't help but sneer at johnny-come-latelys with an "I told you so" under my breath.

Now, with *The Dream Calls For Blood* released on October 11 this year, the band have returned to silence the naysayers for a seventh time. If *Relentless Retribution* showcased their ability to bludgeon, this latest album proves it's their modus operandi. With each track as skull crushing as the one before it, it's quite comforting to know the masters will never be outdone by the students. I can't help but listen to it with a smile on my face, pleased at myself, most of all, for hitting a bullseye after I decided to champion their star when I was just a wee pipsqueak.

To this day, the band have an overarching presence in my life. Whenever I sit down to write one of these Huff Post columns or pick up my guitar to write a rock riff, my autographed Death Angel *Frolic* band promo photo hangs framed above my work desk as motivation. They were one of the bands I can count on two hands that played a big part in motivating me to do what I do today and their inability to falter in my eyes is still a huge inspiration.

However, one must be careful of what is wished for. Because despite my job taking me all over the world to play music, the disappointing repercussion is I'll be missing their Toronto show on November 4 due to my own band's demanding tour schedule. Missing a show might be a small price to pay for most, but when it comes to Death Angel and me, it ain't that easy. You see, we got history.

A version of this piece originally appeared Oct. 28, 2013 on the Huffington Post website

I DON'T CARE THAT IT'S YOUR BIRTHDAY

Regardless if you're a fan of the band or the television show, through social media, I've found that a lot of people suffer from a mild case of arrested development—the disorder whereby the brain ceases to grow and advance. A lot are mild cases and hardly detectable. One has to pay close attention to see the evidence, but when found it stares at you like a deer caught in headlights. I'm talking about the constant need people have, left over from childhood, for others to wish them "Happy Birthday."

Every fucking day on Facebook I am reminded, inundated rather, by prompts telling me that it's so-and-so's birthday. It's become almost obligatory, no matter how much more of an acquaintance than actual friend they are, to visit their Facebook page and leave a complimentary "Happy Birthday, Geraldine!" or "Here's to you on your special day, Pino!" salutation. When you do finally make that trek over to their shitty Facebook page, you find that you're the 67th person to wish them "Happy Birthday" and it's not even 8 a.m.

The "Happy Birthday" ritual gets 100 times worse when you sing for a living in nightclubs like I do. Mix alcohol with someone's desperate need to be validated because they breathed long enough they amassed another year on this planet and it gets so pitiful one needs to avert their eyes. Having to listen to over-eager drunk people tell me it's their birth-day or their friend's birthday and "Could I wish them 'Happy Birthday' from the stage during the show?" is almost as torturous as actually uttering "Happy Birthday" from the stage. I am most proud to say that I've never kowtowed to any of their requests. Watching a six-year-old tear up because you refused their birthday wish is unbearable, but watching a 28-year-old pout because of it is delightful!

It wouldn't be so annoying, but with seven billion people on the planet and only 365 days in the year that means that every day at least one person somewhere has a birthday. It seems to me that having a birthday isn't all that special. In fact, it's probably more worthy to celebrate a good shit than a birthday. A lot of folks don't experience successful bowel movements as often as one would think, especially with today's negligent diets. But everyone, without exception, has a goddamn birthday.

It's a day of respite for the birthday boy/girl, too. People don't get fired or served divorce papers on their birthday. People don't get yelled at or get made to do household chores on their birthday because it's their special day. People all over the world, through some earthen instinct, get a one-day pass once a year to just be happy. For the birthday boy/girl, it's worth celebrating, but for the rest of us it's terrible because we have to pick up the slack.

And what if the birthday boy/girl is widely known as a raging asshole? Then this day of otherwise customary celebration turns into one of dreaded tongue biting as you and everyone around you attempt to spit out "Happy Birthday" through clenched teeth and affected smiles. Because of this time-honoured tradition we end up celebrating the day these slimeballs arrived on Earth to annoy, abuse and antagonize us.

Let's face it, if you're over 16 years old and need to have people fret and fuss over you because it's your birthday, you need to be highly medicated. I'm endlessly fascinated and repulsed by grown adults who expect to be doted over on their birthday like they were nine years old, almost demanding presents, well-wishes and cake. When you watch a 45-year-old blow out the candles on their low-fat cupcake, it's like watching the inverse of a toddler beauty pageant.

Having to slavishly work towards making somebody else feel special 364 days a year is drudgery. Birthdays are making all our lives a living hell. If we did away with the obligatory birthday rigmarole in favour of the morale of the greater good, I bet we'd all live longer and consequently avoid even more birthday wishes because of it!

Don't get me wrong. This isn't some curmudgeonly harangue. I have no problems with getting older. In fact, I've noticed the older one gets, the easier it is to assume the delightful role of "wise" and "all-knowing," whether the title is deserving or not. I've also noticed that as people grow older they can rant, complain and bellyache without much reprimand and that's good to know for the future since I am someone who is full of rants, complaints and bellyaches.

I know what you're thinking: so when is his birthday anyway? To that I say, haven't you learned anything about me yet? I don't care if my birthday is this week and that I want a new iPad, terabyte iPod and the new Ghost B.C. album on gatefold red or yellow vinyl.

A version of this piece originally appeared July 19, 2013 on the Huffington Post website

DANKO'S ULTIMATE STONER MIXTAPE

Being in a rock 'n' roll band gets you scrutinized by people in the straight-laced world very quickly. They immediately assume you're some drug addict and, if you're like me—a person who doesn't drink or smoke— assume you're a recovering drug addict. Truth is, I never had much of a taste for it. I was also lucky enough to get copies of Minor Threat and Bad Brains albums when I was a very impressionable teenager and combing through the lyrics of songs like "Attitude," "Out Of Step" and "Straight Edge" had an indelible effect on me that I am only now starting to recognize.

Despite these beginnings, like a lot of people, I was curious about drugs. I definitely experimented, dabbled, even habitually enjoyed them for some time, and had a general all-around blast. Nobody got hurt and there was never any silly high school drama attached to it. It was only when friends around me overindulged in alcohol did the drama start flowing like a corny after-school special. I never really had the stomach for much alcohol.

Eventually, I knew my time with light drugs had reached its inevitable end and I quietly unrolled the joints, so to speak. Some people have peanut allergies or a fear of heights; I simply couldn't handle my high.

There wasn't any poignant meltdown predicating the decision. OK, maybe I'm somewhat of a control freak. Still, I'm not against it.

But while I've abstained from smoking even an occasional joint, don't think for one second that I don't get a clamouring to grab it every time it's casually passed around me. Much the same way a lactose intolerant pizza lover feels a hunger pang every time the aroma of a slice hits their nostrils, I too feel the sting of a lost puff between my lips from a flaming joint. And even though I don't smoke anymore, my support for the legalization of cannabis is absolute. For anyone interested in learning the true story behind cannabis, I highly suggest watching *The Union: The Business Behind Getting High* by Brett Harvey and Adam Scorgie from 2007.

My main reason for smoking marijuana in the first place was only to enjoy the music I already loved so much, but at a heightened level. It's true that marijuana can open dormant senses and when applied to music the results are unquestionably fantastic. Songs that I'd heard almost a hundred times over suddenly sparkled with nuances that opened up to me like a gift on Christmas morning. Songs that I couldn't quite understand what all the fuss was about suddenly became illuminated pieces of wonderment. Conversely, pot was somehow also able to discern shallow, trite music and instantly made it unbearable. My drug usage had an indisputable effect on how I heard music forever and increased my love for music tenfold.

It's only now when I listen to music sober that I know what a bitter pill I've swallowed after choosing to forego even the occasional smoke. When I see people freely puffing and using it for expanded music listening, I am struck with envy because I know what I'm missing. Still, there are songs that are so close to the feeling I got while on pot that they're almost contact highs by default. I've assembled a mixtape list in order for the uninitiated to get a feel for the magic—and for those who "know," put this list on and just enjoy, you lucky bastards.

Mercury Rev "Chasing A Bee" (from *Yerself Is Steam*/1991)
Easily the best song to start any sort of audio trip.

Donna Summer "I Feel Love" (from *I Remember Yesterday*/1977)
Close your eyes and let this song take you to a place where disco never sucked.

Kyuss "Odyssey" (from *Welcome To Sky Valley*/1994)
Any track off the record would suffice, but this one has the word "mountain" sung by John Garcia. It's hard to pass up.

Jesus Lizard "Then Comes Dudley" (from *Goat*/1991)
Easily one of the greatest tracks to feature the guitar stylings of Duane Denison, one of the most underrated, overlooked guitarists of a generation.

Slint "Nosferatu Man" (from *Spiderland*/1991)
Most would choose "Good Morning, Captain," but that's just too damn depressing when trying to assemble a contact high mixtape.

Hella "Try Dis . . ." (from *Chirpin Hard*/2005)
Probably the one track on this list that comes closest to the raw audible trip all on its own.

Wu-Tang Clan "Clan In The Front" (from *Enter The Wu-Tang*/1993)
This, like most RZA produced tracks, comes alive with substance assistance.

Funkadelic "Maggot Brain" (from *Maggot Brain*/1971)
If you start weeping while listening to this song and you're totally sober then congrats 'cause you're halfway there.

The Rolling Stones "Heaven" (from *Tattoo You*/1981)
The hidden gem from arguably their last great album.

John Coltrane "Olé" (from *Olé Coltrane*/1961)
Pretty hard not to contemplate your entire life listening to this 18-minute opus of bliss.

Shakti "Joy/Lotus Feet" (from *Shakti*/1976)
Another song(s) to bask in its sweet rapture.

Monster Magnet "Tab . . ." (from *Tab* EP/1991)
This song is a journey.

Chrome "SS Cygni" (from *Alien Soundtracks*/1977)
One of the best riffs to hear with or without the aid of dope.

Can "Yoo Doo Right" (from *Monster Movie*/1969)
Sitting and listening to the full 20 minutes of this song is a good antidote
to the three-minute pop song world we all inhabit.

Royal Trux "The Spectre" (from *Cats And Dogs*/1993)
The perfect elixir to a bad day, a bad trip, a bad time.

Rush "Jacob's Ladder" (from *Permanent Waves*/1980)
Rush's diverse fandom can be distilled down to a few songs like this one.

Outkast "SpottieOttieDopaliscious" (from *Aquemini*/1998)
You don't need to be stoned to fall in love with this song, but it would
seriously help.

Neil Young "Cowgirl In The Sand" (from *Everybody Know
This Is Nowhere*/ 1969)
I see this song as the audio equivalent of a relaxant.

Fu Manchu "Blue Tile Fever" (from *King Of The Road*/1999)
If you've made it to this song you're either too high to press stop or
soberly sleeping.

A version of this piece originally appeared Feb. 9, 2013 on the
Huffington Post *website. Illustration by Damian Abraham*

IT'S A LONG TIME 'TIL THE AFTERPARTY ENDS (IF YOU WANNA GO HOME)

Most people who go to rock shows and manage to make their way backstage have no idea of the protocol that exists when being ushered into a band's inner sanctum. Most assume that it's a riotous dionysian meltdown. Maybe it is for bands who only tour on the weekends, but once past the novice stage of road life, most bands, regardless of genre, use the time after the show to reflect, drink in and enjoy the short silence before the merry round of well-wishers make their way backstage.

Some people are nice and only want to wish the band a congratulatory salutation, get an autograph or a pic and be on their way, but there are others, usually people who know nothing about the band, that end up disrupting what can usually be a good hang. Sometimes a good rowdy time gets had by all present, but that's determined by who shows up, what city they're in, how well the show went down, and the mood of the band and crew. You can force a soiree, but it'll usually get stale and awkward very fast.

The first move you, as reluctant host, are expected to make is to offer all who arrive backstage a beer. The band wanted this post-show time to relax and take a shower. But no such luck. You played your balls off and now you must begin hosting a party. By the time it's in full swing, you'll know 35 per cent of the people present and being far from home, end up spending more time watching your belongings to make sure they don't get stolen than having a good time.

During one of these nights on a recent tour, we ran out of beer on the rider quicker than expected. It caused much disappointment for all guests present and everything quickly came to a standstill while I played air drums near the stereo blissfully unaware. This prompted me to turn to our tour manager and ask, "If beer was eliminated from rock 'n' roll, how many people would still be left?"

I don't really drink. I'll have a glass of wine with dinner every once in awhile, but it'll be a few sips to participate in a toast and then a few sips to enjoy the main course. That's it. I've always been very sober during every hang-out, after-party or debauched mess our band has been part of for all these years. I'm usually the one who has to walk over these people at the end of the night, too. Listening to drunk people yap on about absolute nonsense for hours should've earned me a medal by now.

I'm well aware that alcohol aids in lowering inhibitions, makes people more gregarious, adds to the celebratory nature of rock 'n' roll and keeps the clubs that house the music in business. I also understand that over the years people have been brought up to accept alcohol as an intrinsic requirement to the rock 'n' roll experience. With all the importance placed on these drinks and the grave disappointment in people's eyes when it's absent, it always manages to turn the one thing that brought everyone together to begin with—the rock music—into a third place consolation prize (after the sex and drugs).

Maybe I'm an oddity, but I've never needed any chemical help to appreciate rock. I love listening to rock music stone cold sober. It makes me wonder: all the people who need alcohol with their rock music, do they secretly hate it when they're sober? Do they merely tolerate it in order to partake in the social aspect that comes with the rock 'n' roll experience? Does the alcohol become some audio equivalent to what is known as "beer goggles"? Is rock music mostly regarded as some background music to a drinking session, like some youth-tinged version of elevator music? Am I the only one who likes it for real?

The look on people's faces every time I tell them I play in a rock 'n' roll band for a living but don't drink confirms all these queries. It's a look that says it's impossible to listen to rock without being impaired.

So I've finally figured out everyone's dirty little secret: much like their secret stash of porn, most people, even the people who attend rock festivities, privately *hate* rock music.

Fair enough.

The dwindling popularity of rock music on places like the Billboard charts confirms this badly kept secret as rap, country and folk music take over the pop culture landscape. Watching rock music sputter and flail can be hard, but I'm fine with this. At least I'll know the few people left listening to rock are there for the right reasons. That, at least, is something worth raising a glass for.

A version of this piece originally appeared June 14, 2013 on the Huffington Post *website*

THE LINER NOTES FOR SACRIFICE'S FORWARD TO TERMINATION REISSUE

I'm from Scarborough, Ontario, a suburb of Toronto and coincidently where Sacrifice originate. Whether people know or not, when you grew up in Toronto and got into rock music you couldn't help but be inundated with all things Rush—Rush were on the radio every five minutes, there'd be sightings of Geddy Lee at Mac's Milk. Hell, even the house I grew up in is in their "Subdivisions" video (it's the tracking shot along Fundy Bay Blvd. with scenes in L'Amoureux Collegiate). Rush Army Membership kind of came with the postal code and they were definitely a worthy band to hitch your carriage to. But they weren't *my* band. They represented another generation. I needed a band that represented me. That's when I discovered Sacrifice.

I was torturously shy in my adolescent years, preferring to stay in my room and listen to records rather than venture out to shows (to be honest, not much has changed). Only when I had finally saved enough money would I hop on the subway to College Station, go down on Carlton Street to the Record Peddler and buy metal records. Coming home from one such excursion, I had Sacrifice's *Forward To Termination* under my arm, purchased strictly out of civic duty having read Metal Blade ads for *Torment In Fire* describing it as "thrash from Canada." I was blown away by Joe Rico's scorching leads, Rob Urbinati's throaty growl and a musical prowess that exceeded most thrash metal out there at the time. It all made for a sound that's so widely aped by newer bands nowadays they probably don't even know whom they're ripping off. It even contained a "hit" in "Reanimation."

When I found out they were from Scarborough, I enlisted in their army. Just knowing that something of substance could arise from Scarborough's cardboard cutout suburban wasteland (as accurately portrayed in said "Subdivisions" video) gave me a glimmer of hope that you could take this rock 'n' roll thing and put it out onto the world's stage.

These days when I'm traveling around in my own band, I proudly wear my Sacrifice fandom on my sleeve. My heart has leaped with pride whenever someone, upon finding out I'm from Toronto, immediately asks if I've heard of Sacrifice. The loyalty some feel for their favourite sports team is the same loyalty I have for Sacrifice. Maybe I lack the ability to be objective when it comes to the band but *Forward To Termination* doesn't sound dated to me. Probably because I listen to it the way others routinely listen to *Moving Pictures*. Sometimes, when weeks on the road cause an almost incurable case of homesickness, the only remedy is hearing Rob Urbinati yell out "TERMINATE MEEEEEEEEEEEEEEEEE!!!!!!!!!!!!"

This was written for the reissue of Sacrifice's Forward To Termination *album on Cyclone Empire Records*

I MET BETH

FROM THE SONG "BETH", BY KISS OFF THEIR ALBUM "DESTROYER", SUNG BY DRUMMER PETER CRISS. IT WAS THEIR BIGGEST HIT.

SYMPHONIC SOUNDS PRODUCED BY BOB EZRIN, IT'S A BALLAD OF A MUSICIAN WISTFULLY SINGING TO HIS GIRLFRIEND/WIFE, DESPERATELY WANTING TO COME HOME BUT UNABLE TO DO SO. HER NAME WASN'T BETH, IT WAS LYDIA, PETER CRISS' WIFE AND I MET HER.

WHEN YOU'VE EXHAUSTED YOUR FANDOM ON THE OBJECT/PERSON IN QUESTION, YOU EITHER LOSE INTEREST OR GRADUATE TO DIEHARD FAN. YOUR OBSESSION MUTATES INTO A FASCINATION FOR THE MINUTIAE SURROUNDING SAID OBJECT D'AMOUR.

FOR A ROCK FAN, IT MIGHT BE AN EXHAUSTIVE KNOWLEDGE OF THE PRODUCERS, MANAGERS, AND ROADIES OF THEIR FAVOURITE ROCK BAND. SOMETIMES, THE INTEREST IN THE BAND'S MUSIC GETS SUPERSEDED BY THE BEHIND-THE-SCENES TRIVIALITIES THEMSELVES. I AM ONE OF THOSE KINDS OF KISS FANS.

MY FANDOM FOR KISS WILL REMAIN WITH ME FOR THE REST OF MY LIFE, BUT I DON'T LISTEN TO "DETROIT ROCK CITY" OR "I WAS MADE FOR LOVIN' YOU" ANYMORE. HOW MANY TIMES CAN YOU LISTEN TO "ROCK AND ROLL ALL NITE" WITHOUT EVENTUALLY WANTING TO SLIT YOUR WRISTS?

MAINTAINING FANATICISM FOR GENE SIMMONS AND PAUL STANLEY IS SIMILAR TO TRYING TO SUSTAIN INTEREST IN SUPERMAN AND BATMAN AFTER YOU'VE DISCOVERED WOLVERINE, MOON KNIGHT, SPECTRE, AND HAWKMAN.

MEETING LYDIA WAS A HUGE MOMENT FOR ME. SHE HAS AN INSIDER'S VANTAGE POINT THAT ISN'T SKEWED BY AN EGO BUILT OF FAME AND FORTUNE. MORE IMPORTANTLY, SHE BELONGS TO A VERY ELITE CLASS OF PEOPLE, THE MUSE TO ONE OF POPULAR MUSIC'S GREATEST SONGS OF ONE NAME TITLES I.E.

AS SOMEONE WHO HAS HARNESSED MUSES FOR CREATIVE INSPIRATION BEFORE, FINDING THE NUB OF THE SONGWRITER THROUGH HIS/HER MUSE IS AN ELUSIVE AND FUTILE TASK.

SOMETIMES A MUSE IS THERE TO EMOTE ONLY A FEELING. WHEN THE SONG IS OPEN, UPFRONT, AND ABOUT BOUNDLESS LOVE LIKE "BETH" IT PIQUES CURIOSITIES. I HAD TO MEET LYDIA.

WE MET IN MY MANHATTEN HOTEL ROOM, WHILE ON TOUR, TO RECORD A CONVER-SATION FOR MY PODCAST. I WAS NERVOUS. HERE WAS A WOMAN WHO HAD IN-TURN INSPIRED A THOUSAND FIRST/LAST DANCES, ACCOMPANIED MANY A LONELY HEART AND REPRESENTED THE LONGING FOR WHAT COUNTLESS OTHERS WERE GOING THROUGH.

TRUTHFULLY, I ONLY GREW TO LOVE THE SONG WHEN I WAS FAR FROM HOME ON TOUR AND CAUGHT MYSELF SAYING OVER THE PHONE THAT I "CAN'T COME HOME RIGHT NOW" TOO.

ALL MY FEARS AND NERVOUSNESS QUICKLY DISSIPATED WITHIN THE FIRST FIVE MINUTES OF MEETING LYDIA. SHE WAS DISARMING, CHARMING, AND APOLOGETIC FOR BEING ONLY TWO MINUTES LATE.

SHE HAPPILY ENDURED MY INCLINATION TO STEER THE CONVERSATION BACK TO KISS. SHE COURTEOUSLY WENT THROUGH THE ENTIRE BACKSTORY THAT LED UP TO THE RECORDING OF THE SONG, TO HEAR IT FROM LYDIA/BETH WAS INDESCRIBABLE.

THE SECOND PRINTING OF HER BOOK "SEALED WITH A KISS", THE IMPRESSIVE PHOTO BOOK OF HER DAYS MARRIED TO PETER CRISS, HAD JUST BEEN RELEASED AND MEMORIES WERE EASILY REMINISCED.

STORIES I HAD READ TO MYTHOLOGIZING DEGREES WERE CASUALLY TOSSED OFF LIKE THEY HAPPENED YESTERDAY, BUT THIS WASN'T SOME MUSICOLOGIST OR HISTORIAN, THIS WAS THE SOURCE. I WAS IN KISS HEAVEN.

WHEN A BAND OR PERSON ACHIEVE SUPERSTARDOM THE WAY KISS DID, SUPPORTING CHARACTERS TEND TO GET PUSHED ASIDE REGARDLESS OF HOW VITAL THEIR ROLE.

YET, NO MATTER HOW DEIFIED, OVER-EXPOSED, AND STALE THESE MAJOR ACTS GET, IT IS AT THESE MOMENTS WHEN THE TIDE SHIFTS AND THESE BACKGROUND PLAYERS START TO COME TO THE FOREFRONT TO ASSUME THEIR RIGHTFUL PLACE AS DIAMONDS IN THE ROUGH.

LYDIA IS THAT DIAMOND.

Illustration by Fiona Smyth

YOU SHOULD BE ALLOWED TO PUSH PEOPLE

To a large part of Canada, Toronto is seen as a place filled with rude, cold-hearted, selfish people. It's a place where no pleasantries are exchanged. It's a place to live only if loneliness and rat races make you happy. Its sprawling cityscape and adjacent suburban wasteland are viewed as desecrations to the environment. It's a canker desperately trying to play catch-up to New York City but failing miserably. It's a boil on the otherwise upstanding reputation of Canada.

I agree with every fiery postulation about the city. That's why I love it and call Toronto my home.

I feel like apologizing to all the citizens of all the other provinces every time I hear a visiting person make a crack about how people in Toronto will actually scowl at you when they pass you in the streets because you're walking too slow. That was probably me out on one of my daily strolls. Sorry, but you were in my way.

Now I realize the population density of Toronto doesn't come close to places like New Delhi, Tokyo or New York, but considering Canada is the second largest country in the world with almost 10 million square kilometres of land and only 33 million people to nest in it, Toronto's 5.5 million citizens can seem to other Canadians like an overflowing animal cage. Born and raised in Toronto, I have watched the population rise and it certainly feels that way.

But we all have to live with one another and all are welcome. I'm proud of the fact that Toronto is the most multicultural city in the world per capita and we live in relative racial harmony. So if people scowl and aren't the most outgoing and friendly, instead of taking it as an insult and a reason to dismiss the entire city, maybe it can be viewed as the normal defensive tactic used when making your way through the denseness of a city that by sheer numbers only yields isolation as a byproduct.

With Toronto's growing population, I've naturally acquired a set of new pet peeves. One of them is that I can't stand it when people stand in doorways. Doorways are meant to be *passed through*. When you pass through a doorway, chances are there's another person right behind ready to do the same thing. The same can be said of standing at the bottom of escalators. If you just stand there, you block everybody's path and are suddenly barring everyone else from going forth and living the rest of their lives.

Over the years I have quietly contained my anger every time one of these self-absorbed morons obstructs my path. I usually just squeak out an "excuse me" in my politest Canadianese and the person always moves aside, sometimes apologetic, which is nice, but usually still oblivious and operating on a robotic need to avoid further confrontation.

We've all seen these dunces, absorbed in their thoughts, unable to see the other people inhabiting the world around them. They are the centre of their own universe, except their universe is the size of a Frisbee, filled with question marks, and they look like a deer in headlights.

There needs to be drastic steps taken to stop this foolish behaviour.

When someone is caught standing in any publicly used doorway, the person behind them should be allowed to legally push them in order to make them move. The push should be firm, but light. Think of it as the urban version of a herding dog driving the dumb cattle over rugged topography. A push is all you need in order to allow people to keep moving on with their vibrant lives. Holding them back by foolishly blocking a doorway keeps others at a standstill and that should be punishable.

Sure, if actually implemented there will be the tendency for people to push harder than permitted. Some will take advantage of the "push allowance" and turn it into more of a "shove" or a "wallop," but so be it. Fights will break out, but those would be understandable transitionary repercussions and mostly temporary until we settle back into our polite Canadian dispositions.

Of course, I don't think the push rule should be applied to the elderly or small children. And of course there might be disgraceful moments, but it's all par for the course when we embark on the great retraining to teach getting out of people's way and making yourself scarce. "Shove With Love" would become the city's new slogan.

I don't mean for this to be sanctioned and enforced in any other Canadian city, either. Montreal, Vancouver, Calgary, Edmonton, Winnipeg, Halifax and Saskatoon can keep being the friendly and perfectly populated metropolitan areas they've always been. But in order to match the rude reputation that our fair streets of Toronto have acquired there needs to be some follow through, so I say push. Don't push hard, just push. Poke, too.

A version of this piece originally appeared March 16, 2013 on the Huffington Post *website*

KERRY KING MADE ME DO IT

When I was a young whippersnapper, I stood in line early one morning and bought tickets to see Slayer. It was an odd venue to see the band because it was a soft-seater and tickets were distributed by row and seat; there was no general admission. Whoever booked the band at the venue put a lot of faith in us Slayer fans to NOT tear up the seats and destroy the legendary Massey Hall—a venue that has been used to record monumental albums like *Jazz At Massey Hall* by Charlie Parker and Dizzy Gillespie, *Live At Massey Hall 1971* by Neil Young, and, of course, *All The World's A Stage* by Rush.

I showed up at around 8 a.m. on a school day, found out I was third in line and, to my surprise, bought four front row tickets for me and three of my classmates. We were going to see Slayer and we were going to be as close as one could get.

Surprisingly, on the night of the show, there was no barrier and only a handful of security, but nobody moshed, nobody stage-dived and no seats were destroyed. After having the greatest living meltdown of my life, to that point, earlier that evening when I thought I forgot to bring the tickets, I settled back and decided to let it all loose. It was a time in my life when I had little responsibility and no cares in the world. So, standing in one spot, with nothing else to do but watch and listen, I banged my head very hard. It was all I knew to do while Slayer played and I did it at the foot of Kerry King's leather boots.

After the show, the security guard, who was situated right by us, without asking, jumped up on stage, grabbed a Kerry King guitar pick and gave it to me, much to the envy of my classmates. I still have that memento and that moment kicked off my side hobby of collecting guitar picks that I still (occasionally) partake in.

I'm not that committed to the pastime, though. There's been ample times I could've grabbed a pick by a band we were playing with and chose not to bother. Still, I have enough picks that I carefully store them in a mini album normally used for coin collectors and it sits at home alongside other various binders and folders filled with other useless trinkets and knickknacks.

I'm not the only one who does this. I know because I'm always getting asked for a guitar pick by people who like our band. I can only assume they share the same hobby.

Guitar picks are a great item to collect. They're not usually for sale as an official merchandise item, but they're keepsakes that were (in theory) used for the performance of a show. They're vital, intimate utensils and they were usually held by the performers themselves.

However, the one thing that kind of bugs me with the passing of guitar picks between guitarist and audience is the exchange itself.

Guitar picks are small, occasionally, smaller than a penny. When a guitarist throws a guitar pick into the crowd during a live show, do they really expect it to be caught? It's a dark room, filled with strobes and high volume. Unless they're NFL wide receivers or Navy SEALs, how are audience members supposed to catch these plastic chips the size of subway tokens? My guess is most guitar picks thrown into a crowd land on the floor, trampled, forgotten and swept into the garbage along with the rest of the refuse like plastic beer cups and soiled boxer shorts.

The act of throwing guitar picks as a goodwill gesture is a phony parlour trick. It never finds its mark. It's an affected, bullshit pose. Guitar players should stop it.

Now, I'm not saying guitar picks shouldn't be doled out, but they should be handed out one-on-one, eye-to-eye, with dignity. And since it sometimes resembles a communion wafer, receiving one should be a high honour, not something you'll use to pick your teeth with later. If it must be an exchange made during a show to symbolize the connection between band and crowd then it should be distributed as such: individually and with purpose, not randomly and to whosoever has the best ability to track a tiny piece of plastic flying near their head. One must remember that the audience are made up of individuals who need to be specifically addressed rather than grouped together like a pit of snakes in an Indiana Jones movie. Most of the time, however, to the delight of the guitarist's ego, throwing out guitar picks is followed by a demeaning stampede of fanatics hungry to claim it. Ugh!

As much as throwing out drum sticks by drummers at the end of the show can take out an eye, at least you can see the damn thing zinging towards your eyeballs before they get popped out; same with potential mementos like flowers, towels, headbands and other various gadgets used during the standard live rock show. Watching people scramble to snatch something that seems invisible to everyone else is borderline comical.

Most of the time, what people don't realize is the guitar pick they get was discarded without even being played. You might as well hand out 8×10 glossy pics scanned from the internet for all their symbolic significance.

I might not throw out guitar picks during our live shows, but that doesn't mean I'm hoarding them for myself. When someone approaches me for a guitar pick, I reach into my back pocket, where I always keep them, and give them the Dunlop pick with a measured handoff. Most of the time my name has been long rubbed off because I've actually used it. "anko J nes" is the mark of a used live tool, just like a pick reading " layer" sandwiched in the middle of a sworded pentagram feels more real to me than a pristine "Slayer" one.

Of course, the argument can be made that you need to meet the actual players to obtain said item and that's not always easy to do. I understand and agree. Picks shouldn't be something you can buy as a merch item. Guitar picks shouldn't be so easy an item to acquire in order for the damn things to be important. If that's the established standard, maybe, my own collection can start to seem more valuable to people other than just me.

A version of this piece was originally published in the
October 2015 issue of Close-Up Magazine

MEETING ROBIN WILLIAMS

Growing up, rock stars were wild and dangerous, irreverent and outrageous. It's what attracted legions of us to follow them. What charmed me was their courage to perform and ability to master their own madness. It wasn't something I saw around me in my everyday life and it immediately captivated me. Sometimes, their songs were good too.

Comedy was also a place where I froze in wonder and awe. To me, a witty joke, turn-of-phrase, or comedic performance was on par with a great guitar riff or catchy song. When I found out comedians put out records just like rock bands did, I set out to buy as many of them as I could afford. Luckily, this was the time of cassette dubbing and I managed to cull from all my friends' cassette collections, acquiring Steve Martin's *Wild & Crazy Guy,* Cheech & Chong's *Let's Make A New Dope Deal* and Robin Williams' *Throbbing Python Of Love*. I know all these records off by heart, word for word, like "O Canada" or "Happy Birthday."

Throbbing Python Of Love couldn't have come to me at a better time. I was starting to bubble with hyperactive energy and was beginning to have difficulty wielding it. Trying to suppress the non-stop ticker tape of thoughts was quite the task, but listening to Williams go a million times faster on wax . . . relaxed me. The only way to keep up with him was to burrow down, memorize the album and lip sync to it in my room like some wacked-out karaoke party of one.

"What the hell's he doing now? Ha Ha Ha Ha Ha . . . CATCH UP!"

The album is littered with genuine audience outbursts, interactions and heckles which only encouraged Williams to respond and top himself. When someone yells out "Improv!" at the end of side one, Williams snaps, "What do you think the fucking last 30 minutes has been?" Unbridled genius.

So imagine my surprise, 10 or 12 years ago, walking around downtown Toronto, watching a slow figure moving towards me, only to realize it was Williams himself. Needless to say, I was stunned. Little did he know his voice had filled my head for hours that had compounded into days. As we passed each other I could only muster a "Hello, Mr. Williams," to which he politely nodded. Obviously, he wanted to be left alone and that was enough for me.

When I played that moment over and over in my head, I wished it could've gone differently. I realized what I should've said, but thought I'd never get a second chance.

I got my second chance.

One night, after we played a set at the Horseshoe Tavern in Toronto, we got word from our friend John Catucci, the host of *You Gotta Eat Here!*, that Robin Williams was at the Oasis Restaurant on College Street and

about to do an impromptu comedy set in the back room. Even though we were only a few blocks away, we all took cabs over there as fast as we could. We walked in and there he was riffing from the top of his head. Everyone was spellbound. I was in glorious shock. He was hilarious.

After the set, he was semi-mobbed by the scant crowd privy to his "secret" appearance. Of course we all wanted pictures and when I got my turn, I also got my second chance and said, "The first time I saw you I wanted to yell out, 'Joke 'em if they can't take a fuck.'" That was the last line off of *Throbbing Python Of Love.* He then turned to me and said "what a lovely tribute" as the photographer snapped this photo.

The news of Robin Williams passing isn't even 24 hours old. I might be a little emotional right now and cringe at what I've written here later, but Robin Williams came to represent a wildness that I felt a kinship with and carry with me to this day. He was one of a kind.

Robin Williams . . . What A Concept. R.I.P.

A version of this piece originally appeared Aug. 12, 2014 on the Huffington Post *website*

PETER PAN SPEEDROCK— BUCKLE UP AND SHOVE IT!

To me, rock 'n' roll has always stood for freedom. The music was merely the accompanying soundtrack to the attitude. Only through some kind of real-life struggle and hardship can the true rock 'n' roll essence rise to the surface and resonate within the music.

Rock 'n' roll is a loud form of music. It demands attention. These demands have largely been seen as bad form by self-appointed muso-custodians and the genre itself has been widely regarded as lowbrow and deliberately overlooked. With that in mind, continuing to play the music and proudly embody its spirit, despite critical stigma, has an attractive nobility.

I see this quality in Peter Pan Speedrock. Their commitment to a music that isn't widely accepted nor easy to swallow is inspiring. More inspiring still are the songs they play. Rugged precision and finesse is required to play the songs they make. Theirs is a sound that will rip the skin off your face leaving a skull that can only whisper, "More please." It makes you want to enlist in their army, sign up for their squad and join their cause.

I'm a little biased when it comes to trios like Peter Pan Speedrock. Playing in a rock 'n' roll trio myself, I feel a natural kinship to Peter, Bart

N. and Bart G. We all know the distinct intimacy and intensity when there are only three members on stage. It's a balancing act with no net. Born out of a need to compensate for lack of members, rock trios end up being the loudest, the angriest and the hardest.

Peter Pan Speedrock proves my postulation. Their new album *Buckle Up And Shove It!* is everything that has made them infamous around the world. It's rock 'n' roll for the hard-of-hearing. It will give you a hernia, hemorrhoids, diarrhea and make you constipated all at the same time. It will punch you in your teeth, your stomach, your ass and your genitals. It will leave you crippled, knock kneed, decapitated and impaled on a stake.

You're gonna love it.

Danko Jones
April 2014

SURVIVAL OF THE FITTEST

Natural Selection—The process whereby organisms better adapted to their environment tend to survive and produce more offspring. First expounded by Charles Darwin and now believed to be the main process that brings about evolution.—New Oxford American Dictionary

Since the late 1990s, reality shows have taken over almost all of today's television programming. At the helm of this movement was, and still is, the mammoth singing competition called *American Idol*. Franchised all over the world, it has made its winners, judges and even a few losing contestants worldwide stars. The lure of the show is simple and time-less—watching a frog turn into a prince. Everyone loves a rags-to-riches story. Hell, it's the American dream! Who wouldn't want to watch that?

Me, that's who.

There's something to be said for "paying your dues." The only prob-lem is it isn't actually said very often anymore. Even hearing the term roll off my own tongue sounds antiquated. No one uses the term because there aren't any dues to pay. Dues, in the context of professional musi-cians, used to come in the form of slogging it in nightclubs to little acclaim for virtually pennies on the off-chance that something would spark. It was a romantic and, dare I say, even noble pursuit. Today, what has replaced these "dues" are endless line-ups made up of people waiting for a handout and willing to forgo their dignity for 30 seconds of fame in the hopes they won't be laughed at for attempting to sing.

What this new star process yields are anxious, malleable, vacant performers who ape correctly, take instructions obediently and, outside of pleasing the middle of the road, don't have a shred of genuine character. That's not to say they don't have it within them to maybe one day rise above their shallow beginnings, but that rarely happens given the accelerated lifecycle of network television-created pop stars. It's this immediacy within the petri dish of the television studio that produces a hobbling gimp of a star who, within a short period of time, will begin to exhibit injurious recessive genes that inhibit long-term fame. Inevitably, their fate will most likely consist of being eaten and spat back out by the general public, much like one does after eating a half-cooked meat.

What's lost on everybody is that the chase is really better than the catch. It's this gestation period that's fascinating. Taking sometimes years to develop into a quality musician doesn't make for good television. Trying to figure out how to write a proper song took me years! I still don't know how (as a large number of people would most likely concur). Trying to learn how to keep my voice intact over a six- to seven-week tour during the cold months took me eight years! Yes, I'm a slow learner but it's these bitter pills of trial and error in every facet of music that make the journey constantly engaging. There is no rulebook, coach or compassionate audience to seek support from on this side of the music biz and that leaves a lot of people with weaker constitutions out to dry. The true musicians and performers who really persevere after years of slogging it out (beyond an eight-hour wait in a line-up to sing a Diane Warren or Randy Newman song) eventually gain skills in all fields (business, street smarts, songwriting, performing, playing, public relations) that far outweigh their novice reality show counterparts and this shows in their recorded output.

Of course, these singing competitions aren't the whole scope of music, but it's the part that is most celebrated, most lauded over and most known.

The other side, the one I'm familiar with, comes with few perks and relative obscurity. The teeming masses sucking on the *American Idol* teat usually have the lowest common denominator taste in pop culture pap and somehow that doesn't really bother me. They stay on their side of the fence, I stay on mine, and never the two shall meet.

Being the fittest to survive in the jungle of the music business takes someone made of strong stuff. The music business can be as alluring as a tasty guitar riff, or as malodorous as a cheesy melodramatic ballad. It's easy to get sucked in by its charms, but what you need to know is that it's really a canker-ridden, bottom-feeding sodomite of a beast, and the real comedy begins when all the hoopla has faded and the last audience member is shuffled out the television studio. It is precisely at this moment when the newly crowned reality show prince or princess slowly realizes that natural selection has taken over and they sold their soul to a gaudy reality show.

A version of this piece was originally published in Burning Guitars *2011*

DRESSING UP AS VINNIE VINCENT

Dressing up like Vinnie Vincent for kicks.

Recently, I got invited to a costume party. There was no specific theme to the costumes but it was mostly an excuse to celebrate the host's birthday. I hemmed and hawed at who or what or how I was going to dress up. I remembered there being two people from last year's birthday bash who showed up dressed as Slash from Guns N' Roses and another guy dressed as Gene Simmons. There was even a guy who claimed to be James Hetfield circa *Load*, but that's just because he didn't prepare a costume.

I remember how horrible the Gene Simmons costume had been (black jeans and black shirt with wrong make-up design and no widow's peak) and how every year, no matter where you go, there is always some douchebag wrongly dressed up like Gene or Paul and nobody says anything. I mean, how predictable! If, by dressing up like The Demon or The Starchild, you want to show the world you're a huge KISS fan you're going about it the wrong way. I honestly think Ace Frehley's costume is a little more elaborate, and if done correctly, much more impressive. Even more striking would be Peter Criss' Catman outfit circa *Love Gun*, complete with bullet belts or even Eric Carr's debut Fox outfit. Still, I decided to do everyone one better at this party by going out as VINNIE VINCENT!!!!!

There are only six people in the entire world who have had the honour of wearing official KISS make-up designs (Tommy Thayer dressed up as the Spaceman and Eric Singer dressed up as The Catman DO NOT

COUNT). Of course, Gene, Paul, Peter and Ace are the original four, and The Fox, Eric Carr (R.I.P.) is the well-known fifth member, but most people have no idea Vinnie Vincent also served time as the Paul Stanley-designed Ankh Warrior between 1982 and 1983. It was during a brief low period in KISStory but remains nonetheless all real.

Vinnie Vincent left an indelible stamp on KISStory by helping to pen such classics as "I Love It Loud," "Lick It Up," "All Hell's Breakin' Loose" and "Unholy." I chose to go out as Vinnie Vincent this year knowing most people don't know who he is, thus forcing me to explain my costume choice and showing everyone within earshot that it was I, and not these run-of-the-mill Gene Simmons knockoffs, who was the biggest KISS fan of them all.

When it was all said and done, I must be honest, nobody had a clue who I was and nobody bothered to ask me either. I couldn't even fit into the spandex outfit I had bought at the ballerina store near my place so I opted for jeans and a t-shirt, too. Word got around the party that someone was dressed up as an "evil transvestite" and another person was dressed up as famous drag queen, RuPaul. I realized only after the party was over that they were all talking about me. Still, I was very proud of my Vinnie Vincent costume and dare I say have probably been the only KISS fan who has had the balls to dress up like Vinnie when the occasion arose.

I would love it if more KISS fans embraced The Ankh Warrior as much as they love The Demon or The Star Child, so I've decided to demonstrate how to apply The Ankh Warrior make-up with a colorful pictorial in the pages of *Close-Up*.

*A version of this piece was originally published in
the April 2011 issue of* Close-Up Magazine

MUSICIANS TALKING = DANTE'S 9 CIRCLES OF HELL

Are you into S&M? Do you enjoy cock and ball torture? Perhaps you like getting whipped by some dominatrix? Maybe your high threshold for pain stems from some sort of fetishized pleasure of it? Maybe you've exhausted all routes of getting choked, spanked, whipped and cow prodded and are looking for new heights of torment? You want it so painful that you just might pass out? Look no further because I have your new painful pleasure: ask a musician about their music.

Listening or reading about what a musician has to say about their own music is the holy grail of torture. It's the equivalent to getting your leg sawed off without any anesthesia or forcing you to swallow your own eyeballs after they've been pulled out. I have almost poked my own eyeballs out when I've heard the nonsense that comes out of the mouths of these yokels who play five chords on a guitar. If you suddenly walked in the middle of a musician babbling and didn't know what they did for a living or what exactly they were talking about, you'd swear, by the gravity of their tone alone, they were working to save all of mankind. The worst thing is I'm in the same line of work as these assholes.

Don't get me wrong; these kinds of "musicians" aren't charlatans. They *believe* every damn word that comes out of their mouths no matter how condescending or inane it can get. They're just buffoons—coddled, spoiled and patronized village idiots. They actually think their gauche poems, when paired with A, G and B chords, have deep-seated profundity past being something to hum when taking a shower.

Let's take a look at the jargon that they apply when describing themselves and their "music."

When blathering on about songwriting, words like "process," "exploration," "spawn," "accomplish" and "evolving" infer that writing songs requires great toil and works in tandem with their own personal development as a human being, something most people, a.k.a. non-songwriters, will never get to experience. Words like "honesty," "vision" and "inspired" infer that their fragile work is of a divine nature with them acting as holy mediums.

I would love to see how long these spiritualist workhorses would last working in a factory or better still, working cash at a Dunkin' Donuts. I give them half a shift before they all start to implode. But then again, they'd probably run home and write a damn song about it replacing the words "donuts" and "coffee" in the verses with "rawness" and "artistry."

In the greatest betrayal to musicians everywhere, I'm gonna let you in on an industry secret—Penn & Teller style—about what it's like to write songs. You pick up your guitar, piano etc. and play it until something sounds good. It might take five minutes or it might take 50 days. You record it and then, if enough people like the combination of chords you've managed to derivatively cobble together, you might be allowed to do it again.

That's it.

There's no ethereal, otherworldly contact. There's no inward psychic connection. There's no past life regression analysis. There might be a lot of mumbo jumbo, but not much else.

Sure, everyone's allowed to prattle on every once in awhile, myself included (like I'm doing right now). But it's almost a journalistic device similar to watching a spider get tangled in their own web to allow musicians to blather on about their music. It makes for great amusement and confirms them as the halfwits they've long been suspected of being. (I'm also aware that by writing all this I'm ensnaring myself to some degree.)

If yammering on about how much others yammer on paints me into a corner, so be it. Just make sure that if I must get painted in a corner, it's not beside one of these dingbats. Anything except having to listen to them talk about how "deeply personal" whatever it was they just did made them "push boundaries."

A version of this piece originally appeared Feb. 16, 2013 on the Huffington Post *website*

ONLY TRUST IOMMI

"You can only trust yourself and the first six Black Sabbath albums."
—Henry Rollins

The above quote has recently gained a lot of ground on social media platforms and come to almost encapsulate the band, and even heavy metal as an entire genre. I've seen the quote branded on t-shirts worn by kids who weren't even born when the Birmingham, England innovators released *Forbidden*. The thing is, the more people read this line, and the more it's said, the more it becomes a stark molten rock truth.

There are two aspects about the quote that can never be disputed: 1) Black Sabbath's self-titled debut album from 1970 essentially invented heavy metal and gave rise to a movement that launched a thousand bands. 2) Henry Rollins, the man who coined the buzz-quote, has long been known to be a Black Sabbath super-supporter and aficionado.

However . . . and I say "however" with a punctuated ellipsis because I'm gonna use this space I've been given in *Close-Up* to REFUTE the above quote. It's scary to do so as I'm sure it will only invite a barrel of yahoos armed with pitchforks and torches on my front lawn ready to burn me at the stake, but read carefully because I feel you can only trust yourself and ALL 19 BLACK SABBATH ALBUMS.

That's right, 19 fucking albums! I bet there's a lot of people reading this that didn't even know Black Sabbath recorded 19 albums. When a band is four decades old, there will be shifts and turns, peaks and valleys, moments of bewilderment and brilliance in their history and one must look at their entire body of work. If each is graded by their best work as the yardstick then there will most certainly be diminishing returns. Rather, each album should be graded as its own entity, since we're talking about a discography that spans 43 years.

To cut off the 43 year-old Black Sabbath discography at its knees by giving import to only its first six albums is dismissing records like *Heaven And Hell*, *Technical Ecstasy*, *Mob Rules*, *Seventh Star*, *Born Again* and *The Eternal Idol*. It's a veritable slap in the face, slanderous to the brand of Black Sabbath and its legacy. Dismissing "Zero The Hero," "Die Young," "Neon Knights" and "Turn Up The Night"? Are you fucking kidding me?

Am I to believe that Sabbath held no sway past 1975? Are we saying Sabbath were only good for five years? Is the seventh album, *Technical Ecstasy*, really that bad? Maybe the album's artwork deserves a trouncing, but definitely not the tracks contained within like "Backstreet Kids," "All Moving Parts (Stand Still)" or the Ward-sung classic, "It's Alright." I refuse to drink the Kool-Aid on this issue, ladies and gentlemen.

I believe Rollins uttered it to relay a greater point—that Sabbath are worthy of your attention and to never to take them for granted. After all, Rollins has praised *Heaven And Hell* in the past. He's also praised their recent reunions. Maybe it was expressed casually and demanded no further weight past the moment it was said. If this is the case, why choose this quote from all of Rollins' quotes about Black Sabbath as the clarion call for a movement/genre/generation?

"Trust" is a big word these days. It's a word that a lot of people feel is hard to find anywhere and in anyone. I am in agreement. When someone/something is deemed trustworthy, people tend to flock to it, stand by it and rely on it. Are Black Sabbath trustworthy? Absolutely, if getting your ass kicked by music is what one seeks. But one's trust in Black Sabbath cannot and should not be limited to the first six albums. Let those 13 other albums grace your life with their presence. Let go of any preconceived hangups or anxieties when it comes to their line-up changes, musical shifts and productions. You don't have to love all of them, but goddammit you can't only love six.

What needs to take hold is a newer Black Sabbath rallying cry. One that encompasses all members, all eras, all albums faithfully. Maybe I can coin it here in the pages of *Close-Up*?

Here it is . . .

ONLY TRUST IOMMI

What do you think?

I think it's perfect. It sounds catchy by playing off the words "only" and "Iommi" rhyming together and sharing the same cadence. It isn't era-specific either. It doesn't pick Ozzy over Dio or Cozy Powell over Bill Ward or Tony Martin over Glenn Hughes or Geezer Butler over Neil Murray. It doesn't admonish anybody or anything, but rather gives credit and praise to the one person who has been there from beginning to end, thick and thin—Tony Iommi.

Can you hear that sound? That's the sound of a thousand t-shirt presses slapping that phrase on a thousand t-shirts. Save me one, would ya?

A version of this piece was originally published in the August/ September 2016 issue of Close-Up *Magazine*

STOP SINGING "HALLELUJAH" SO MY EARS CAN STOP BLEEDING

There are millions of songs out there. Some are good and some aren't so good. Yet, with as many songs that exist and the amount of new songs being written every day you'd think people's knowledge and recall of them would be vast to the point of discombobulating. Apparently not so. In this society, when it comes to determining one's hierarchy of needs, music is treated as an afterthought, an addendum, audible wallpaper.

Most people have a mental reserve of only a few thousand songs culled from childhood and their teen years before they reach adulthood and stop experiencing new music. This disconnect people have on a personal level strikes me as strange considering music's intrusion on our personal space every day in shopping malls, sports stadiums, doctor's offices, television commercials, on telephones and in elevators. On second thought, it's most likely backlash because of it.

Through it all, like sperm breaking into the inner sanctum, some songs have an odd resoluteness that crash through racial, class and generational barriers and are destined to live in our psyches forever. Trust me, even the darkest, most evil black metalhead, if held at gunpoint, will be able to stumble through a half-sung version of USA For Africa's "We Are The World" or Britney Spears' "Hit Me Baby One More Time."

Conversely, the most down hip-hop head, if faced with being waterboarded, will be able to sing the chorus of "Smells Like Teen Spirit" or "Enter Sandman" like it was "Happy Birthday." Some of these songs, however beloved they were upon first entering the pop culture milieu, will gradually become disliked due to excessive rotation. There was a time, long, long ago, when Led Zeppelin's "Stairway To Heaven" sounded great. Sadly, those days are long behind us and encountering that song now means eight minutes of your life you'll never get back.

As the days roll by, and more treasured songs become reviled with their unwelcomed anointment into our lives, I find myself zeroing in on certain songs with abhorrence while allowing others a pass. For example, I don't mind hearing Rihanna's "Umbrella" because I think she's hot and it's still fairly new. But the recent rediscovery and exhumation of Leonard Cohen's "Hallelujah" should cease and desist immediately.

I'll admit I love the song, or should I say *loved* the song. As much as Cohen wrote it, John Cale's version is the beautiful template from which Jeff Buckley parroted to perfection on his superb 1994 album *Grace,* a scant 10 years after Cohen's recording. I have yet to hear a version of "Hallelujah" that bests it and trust me, everyone and their grandmother have been falling over themselves almost desperate to show the world they can sing it.

Everyone from Bon Jovi, Axel Rudi Pell, Bono, Tangerine Dream, Willie Nelson, k.d.lang to even Adam Sandler have performed and/or recorded it. There are hundreds of others who've taken their stab at it and it always sucks balls. Slowly, as each new take on "Hallelujah" has hit my ears, my initial fondness for the song has devolved into absolute loathing.

After Buckley did it back in 1994, covers of "Hallelujah" should've stopped (just like George Lucas should've after *Episode VI*). However, we're talking about the music biz, a hollow-hearted juggernaut that thrives on redundancy, or "heavy rotation" as it's been coined. Whether it's repeating the same catchy chorus in a song over and over again,

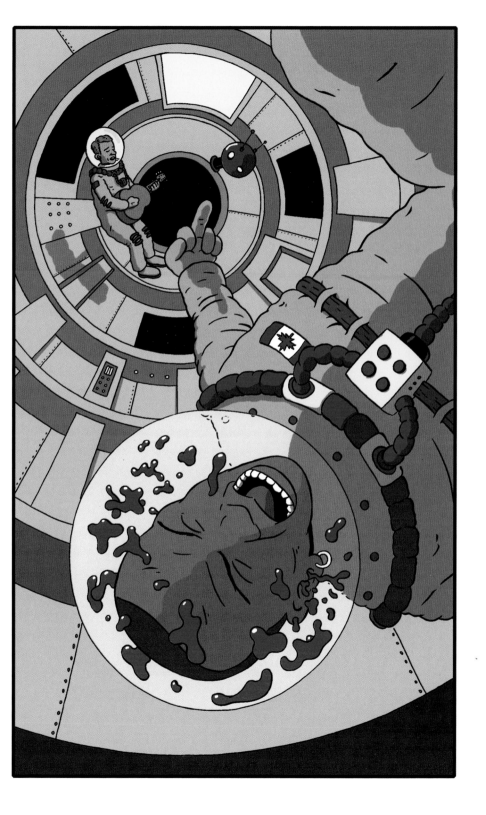

signing bands/singers that ape the most popular acts, or hearing your once-favourite song on the radio a million times over, popular music has been streamlined to deaden your insides.

For the singer, I understand the song's appeal. In our secular world, it's the closest to being a religious hymn, something a lot of people quietly yearn for, whether they realize it or not. Usually sung at a high register in hushed tones, this song about a man's struggle with himself/God/partner/love/lust etc., endows the singer with an angelic, ecclesiastical stature upon delivery. It almost demands reverence from an audience, even after horrible renditions. So it makes sense its appeal to the parade of soulless, attention-starved egos lurking in the rock 'n' roll biz is unparalleled.

Just like Cale so resourcefully unearthed this buried song from the depths, so should someone else pick up the gauntlet and troll the vast library of songs out there to liberate another gem to the forefront. And then it too might grow to become a celebrated tune synonymous with revulsion and nausea. Anything to stop the endless procession of gimp-like "Hallelujah" covers.

Never will it be more appropriate to utter the title of the song out loud than on the day the final "Hallelujah" cover is sung. "Hallelujah!" I will shout from the highest mountain, "My ears can stop bleeding and I can now take the forks out of my eyes."

A version of this piece originally appeared Oct. 15, 2013 on the Huffington Post *website. Illustration by Cam Hayden*

SECRET LETTERS TO RITCHIE BLACKMORE

(Around 2007 I started writing letters to Deep Purple's Ritchie Blackmore. I'd write them and read them out loud to the guys in the van mainly to kill some time while travelling long hours out on the open road to the next gig. The more I'd write them, the more they would dare me to mail them off. So, eventually, I did. I never got a response because they're obviously a joke, but here are a few for you to read.)

June 9, 2007
Long Beach, California, USA
Dear Ritchie,

Do you like watches? I don't think there are enough rock stars who wear them on stage. Can you name any? I sure can't. It's always been a mystery as to how the band knows exactly when to finish their show when there aren't any personal clocks adorned on themselves.

Watches can be cool looking, too. They're usually silver and shiny and give the person on stage something to do. Like look at them. I don't think they get in the way either. Hell, most guys in bands are already wearing some sort of wristband. Why not put a clock on it? Just for your information, that would be called a watch.

So the next time you play a show my suggestion would be to wear a watch. They're snazzy, sophisticated and tell the whole world that you are aware of the time. Plus, it helps prevent going on longer than necessary and this keeps the audience wanting more. All this from a watch!

No, I don't work for a watch company. I'm just a huge fan of watches.

Yours sincerely,

D. Jones

———

September 18, 2007

Winnipeg, Manitoba, Canada

Dear Ritchie,

Have you ever been told that you bear a striking resemblance to famed '70s magician, Doug Henning? Well, you most certainly do. Are you two related in any way? I find it quite peculiar that you like to dress like a sorcerer while he liked to perform magic. You aren't the same person are you? I've never seen the two of you in the same room at the same time and you never guested on any of his NBC television specials either. Interesting. Now that Doug Henning is dead you're everywhere, which is also quite peculiar. Your thoughts?

Yours inquisitively,

D. Jones

———

December 8, 2007

Montreal, Quebec, Canada

Dear Ritchie,

I would love an 8x10 glossy picture of you. Truth is I'm not much of a fan, but I need the photo to prove to people I am not you. Every day, without fail, and for the last seven or eight years, I have been stopped on the street and asked to take a photograph or sign an autograph from people thinking I am you. Although I think you are a handsome man for your age, I find it extremely insulting being mistaken for you because I am a 58-year-old woman and mother of three. In fact, my oldest daughter is pregnant and I will even be a grandmother in a few months. If I had a dollar for every time some guy has asked me how to play a song called "Smoking In The Water" (???) I'd have about $500. It's annoying and I don't even know what they're talking about!

So, I implore you to send me the photo. Don't personalize it or even autograph it. Just send it over and maybe send a few extras. I already know that the amount of times I'm gonna have to whip it out of my purse and prove to people I'm not you will put wear and tear on the photo. I'd probably need a couple of backups. Thanks.

Yours desperately,

D. Jones

———

January 15, 2008
Munich, Germany
Dear Ritchie and Candice,

When you first started Blackmore's Night, I was confused as to why you would want to leave Deep Purple, but upon hearing the first few tracks of *Shadow Of The Moon* I instantly realized why. Blackmore's Night is an all-encompassing musical tapestry that tingles and tantalizes each pleasure point in one's body.

I must say, my wife Jordette and I enjoy your records immensely, and even take them with us when we go on our monthly camping trips with our friends, Cecilia and Joaquin. All four of us are rabid (Advanced) Dungeons & Dragons players and use your records as our soundtrack. I even have my lucky 12-sided crystal die affectionately nicknamed, "Can-Dice." I doubt that I would be where I am now (a 21st-level Half-Elven Cleric with allegiance to Corellon Larethian) without the aid of your fantastic CDs.

Thank you for the wonderful inspiring music.

Yours profusely,

D. Jones

January 17, 2008

Brussels, Belgium

Dear Ritchie,

Are you familiar with the widespread practice of playing Pink Floyd's *The Dark Side Of The Moon* while watching *The Wizard Of Oz* on mute? It seems that the images link up to the sounds on the album, and although the band have never admitted it on record, a growing legion of people are convinced the album was recorded with the intention of syncing the album up with the movie.

All these interesting games had me thinking one night when a very peculiar thing happened as I loaded up my DVD player with some video store rentals, one of which included *Sex And The City*, the movie. My wife and I are huge fans of the HBO television series and I've even gone out and bought the Candace Bushnell book for her birthday, which I guiltily read after she had devoured it. I love Carrie Bradshaw (played by Sarah Jessica Parker) and her fashionista/New York City *je ne sais quoi* friends. Even though they are four upwardly mobile single women discussing their personal lives, I have found similarities with my guy friends and I. For example, my buddy Lance is so Samantha, shagging anything that moves, while all the guys would definitely peg me for Charlotte, which I embarrassingly must concur. I wouldn't call myself a stick-in-the-mud, but I'm definitely more traditional and conservative than the other guys.

Just as I pressed play and sat down to watch Carrie and the girls, our copy of your album, *The Village Lanterne*, which my wife always keeps on repeat throughout our summer house as it blends well with the potpourri and our spice garden out back, started up again on the CD player. The thought flashed through my head to see if both synced together and as both played I couldn't help but notice that there indeed were some suspicious concurrences:

25 Years

1. 27 seconds into the start of the movie Blackmore's Night vocalist Candice Night starts to sing *"25 years since I woke up trembling"* while

a young girl onscreen looks at a pair of shoes in a storefront window. This could stand for a young Carrie and a possible hard early life.

2. *"Tried to run but my feet were frozen"* is sung just as Carrie stops in her tracks after a passing girl on the street compliments her dress.

3. *"Long ago, far away / In the mist of yesterday"* is sung as Carrie sidesteps a young couple having an argument on the street. This could symbolize her emotional and often contemptuous relationship with Mr. Big.

4. As the chorus chimes again, *"Long ago, far away / In the mist of yesterday,"* the audience is shown a summary of the Mr. Big backstory from the television series.

5. As Carrie and Mr. Big condo shop, the elevator door in the building they're viewing closes as the song fades.

Village Lanterne

6. Drums start just as Carrie walks into her prospective penthouse apartment, much like a queen into her court.

7. *"And in that heart I'm with you all along"* is sung as Mr. Big agrees to purchase the penthouse apartment despite the high price tag.

8. *"Bringing me closer to home"* is sung as Carrie is reunited onscreen with her three girlfriends, Charlotte, Miranda and Samantha.

9. An instrumental break in the song allows the movie to showcase some of the jewelry on display at the auction the four women attend.

I Guess It Doesn't Matter Anymore

10. A gloomy song which plays perfectly to Carrie's second-guessing of Mr. Big's intentions. They discuss her reservations and as she shakes her head Candice sings *"I Guess It Doesn't Matter Anymore"*

11. When the scene ends the couple happily embraces and the chorus takes on a more jovial meaning.

The Messenger

12. Reading the morning paper, Charlotte spots Carrie's marriage announcement on page six. Enid, Carrie's editor at *Vogue*, pitches

her "40-Year-Old Bride/The Last Single Girl" piece. These printed announcements are "the messagers."

World Of Stone

13. A choir is heard just as the first shot of Carrie in a wedding dress appears on screen.
14. *"Once a world of glittering hope / This world is not the world we knew"* is sung and meant to foreshadow the wedding fiasco.
15. *"Their lonely eyes haunt me still"* is sung as Samantha is shown happily crying, but quietly sad.
16. *"Good fortune will shine down on us / Together we will win"* is sung as Carrie and Mr. Big settle in bed reading a love letter from Beethoven.

Faerie Queen

17. *"Over on the hill there grows a flower"* is sung as Carrie climbs the steps of The New York Public Library.
18. *"The fairy queen sits there"* is sung as Carrie realizes she wants to be wed at the library.
19. *"Fading with the setting sun"* is sung as Miranda and Steve's marriage is crumbling at the dinner table. *"Help me see / Just one look / She is gone"* is sung after Steve is ignored in the bedroom.

St. Teresa

20. Drums and guitar are introduced as Samantha reaches into her boyfriend Smith Jerrod's pants.
21. *"Reach down for the sweet stuff when she looks at me"* is sung as Samantha watches her male neighbor have sex with a woman.
22. An instrumental break to emphasize Carrie's walk into her new closet.

Village Dance

23. Carrie and the girls each take a turn trying on various dresses from Carrie's wardrobe ending with all girls on the bed.

Mond Tanz / Child In Time

24. *"If you've been bad / Lord I bet you have / And you've been hit by flying lead / You'd better close your eyes and bow your head / And wait for the ricochet"* is played during the scene where Steve admits he's been unfaithful to Miranda.

25. The build-up at the end of the song mirrors the scene where Mr. Big is starting to grow concerned at the enormity of the marriage.

Streets Of London

26. *"Have you seen the old man outside the seaman's mission"* plays as Steve and Miranda talk on the streets of New York.

Just Call My Name (I'll Be There)

27. Candice sings the first half of the chorus on her own, *"I'll be there in the night when you need me / Just call my name"* as Carrie comforts and kisses Mr. Big.

28. *". . . calling me crazy"* is sung as Mr. Big calls Carries cellphone.

29. *"I don't need to know the answers / I don't want to understand / We were born to take the chances / I know the truth when you hold my hand"* is sung while Carrie tries despairingly to calm his pre-wedding jitters. They can almost be her words in the screenplay. In total there are three phone calls onscreen while this song plays.

Olde Mill Inn

30. This is the happiest song on the album and aptly playing while the marriage party gathers and marches to the church.

Windmills

31. The sad acoustic intro is played as Mr. Big tells Carrie he can't marry her and she almost faints.

32. As Mr. Big has yet another change of heart and wants to turn back and marry Carrie *"He battles his shadows and demons / Fighting to light the way"* and *"Still he braves his path."*

Street Of Dreams

33. *"Do you remember me on a street of dreams / Running through my memory on the street of dreams / You are on every face I see on the street of dreams"* plays as Carrie plays back the events of the day and her relationship with her boyfriend and near-husband, Mr. Big.

Really, don't try to convince me that this album wasn't made to accompany *Sex And The City*, even when the moonlit cover of "Village Lanterne" is completely in contrast with the HBO television show's daybreak cover. I know you will probably deny ever even watching an episode of the series, but if I ever meet you in person I'd want you deny it to my face, just so I can see that twinkle in your eye.

Yours Carrie-fully,

D. Jones
P.S. Strangely, this also syncs up with
Eat Pray Love starring Julia Roberts.

CASSETTES MUST BE DESTROYED

Every time I buy three-ply toilet paper I can't help but appreciate the times we live in. It's a decadent feeling wiping your ass on what amounts to mini throw pillows. It's a delicate way to ease into the cold fact that no matter who we think we are, nature is there to remind us we're all equal by constantly making us soil a bowl.

Toilet paper literally holds our hands through this grim process by wrapping around our palms and shielding us from a fecal fiasco. You try not to think that, with every wipe, we are only millimetres away from plopping a shit show onto our own paws and letting the terror take over.

Now imagine a world without toilet paper. Imagine a world where the only way to wipe your ass clean was to wipe your ass with your hands. Many wouldn't care and continue on, but that's only because they haven't given it enough thought. What if you were in the middle of kneading dough or chopping onions or cracking open peanuts? What if the only way to soothe your colicky baby was to get them to suck on your pinky finger and in the middle of it all you had to drop a deuce? The horror would hit you like a ton of bricks.

This is what it's like to have cassette tapes make a comeback in the music biz.

Why anybody would want to own a cassette tape in this post-millennial digital world of ease and functionality is both puzzling and infuriating.

It truly is having access to three-ply toilet paper and opting to wipe your ass with your bare hands. But why stop there? Why use email when one can use a homing pigeon? Why use your camera phone when you can make a pin camera. Why use a car when there's horse and buggy? Why watch television when one can easily fashion a puppet show out of socks and cardboard?

Let's call the cassette revival for what it is—a pose. It's a way of distinguishing yourself from the plebeian masses. It's a way of saying that your taste and your preferences revolve in another strata. The punchline to this way of thinking is cassettes are probably the most inoperable, faulty way of listening to music. They break, they warp, they warble, they unravel and they do not last—a perfect end to a shite medium. For god's sake, one needs a lead pencil just to rewind them! It's the modern day example of the emperor's new clothes.

Before iPods, iPhones and Discmans, there were "Walkmans." They were all the rage. For the first time ever you could conveniently plop a cassette tape into your player and walk around, mobile and free. You could finally have a soundtrack to what you'd see around you. I used it to block out my surroundings and retreat inside my head as I watched the world. However, it would all come crashing down on me when the tape in my Walkman would warp and, rendered musicless, I'd be forced to listen to the sound of the subway or people coughing. It was a low form of going cold turkey and it fucking sucked.

Everybody who has an aggressive hate-on for cassettes went through similar scenarios and, when they were finally phased out by the record biz 20 years ago, we all breathed a sigh of relief. The wicked witch had been crushed by a higher format i.e., compact discs, never to be heard from again . . . until a new generation of clueless bozos decided, despite zero redeeming qualities, cassette tapes should be raised from the dead.

How does one even listen to a cassette tape today? No home electronic store carries cassette players. You have to search online or find someone who is about to throw their old gear out. Our world is a world of digital ease, and before the singularity comes I'm gonna enjoy it, goddammit. Anyone who puts a concerted effort into making it *harder* to listen to music, in my overbearing opinion, doesn't actually like music. I need to have music around me 24 hours a day and the easier that can be facilitated—streaming on my computer, accessed via the cloud, ripped from a flashdrive onto a PS4, whatever—the better.

This recent cassette tape fetish doesn't come close to the parallel resurgence of vinyl. Mainly because vinyl still works! Just ask any person owning a first-pressing copy of Hank Mobley's self-titled 1957 record on Blue Note Records. If cared for properly, vinyl will always be there for one to play and cherish, unlike the Russian roulette game of owning and playing cassettes.

One of a kind, personal recordings of you and/or your loved ones that have been captured on cassette tapes (when you recorded your dad yelling at you and your friends or your grandma singing songs, for example) need to be kept and, on occasion, listened to. This is the only reason that I can think of to hold onto cassette tapes.

But if your wish is to play the new Adele or the new Foo Fighters on cassette when you can easily own an audibly superior version on a different format, you have graduated to the next level of fake poseur and your insecure need to be seen as special and interesting reeks of patheticness. It makes me want to perform a colonoscopy on myself to numb the pain of looking at you.

Basically, fuck off.

MAKE SATAN GREAT AGAIN

The first time I heard Eddie Van Halen I finally relented and gave in to the notion that you didn't need to wear make-up, fancy clothes, or assume some otherworldly alter ego to be taken seriously as a band. In total opposition to every music critic who repudiated flamboyant bands like KISS, as a pre-pubescent know-it-all I held them up as the standard for all other bands to meet. In my child brain, I seriously thought that without make-up you weren't worth your salt as a band, regardless of songs, chops, or stage presence. But as my musical tastes shifted with the years, I found myself conceding and began championing bands that I quietly deemed "plain-looking."

Slowly the idea of incorporating glitz, glamour and make-up into rock 'n' roll grew tiresome for everyone, including me. Especially when the music accompanying it started to seem weak and insincere compared to what these lesser "plain" bands were churning out underground. In the end, the playing field was levelled by punk rock, thrash metal and, eventually, Nirvana. Much to my surprise, I found myself on the opposite side of the music I grew up with as a kid. I felt like a turncoat, but the critically adored music being made by boring looking dudes was undeniably worth backing.

As the years passed, most bands, including KISS, ceded to the idea of dressing down to let the music do more talking than the spectacle. Since

music is subjective and relative to one's surroundings, it can be difficult to conclude if this approach was better for the music, but one thing's for certain: dressing up was critically looked down upon and indelibly relegated to novelty (i.e., GWAR, Green Jelly, Lordi, Insane Clown Posse).

Of course, absence makes the heart grow fonder and as much as music today has splintered into dozens of different genres and factions, there's still a longing from a huge section of the music audience for pageantry and glamour. KISS putting the make-up back on in '96 was a litmus test that proved this to be true. To a degree, at least. Despite releasing three successful albums since their make-up "revival," the band exist mainly in the category of nostalgia these days, albeit at the top of their field.

What this says is I wasn't alone in unconsciously yearning for a time when bands of pomp and ceremony would ascend in popularity again. Sure there were the masked maniacs in Slipknot, but their rise coincided with the popularity of nu-metal, a style of heavy metal that I wasn't very fond of and it took me years to realize that they were anything but. Also, despite my enjoying the music, Slipknot were a band meant for another generation and I couldn't relate to the overall image. I needed a band that spoke to me not just musically, but conceptually.

Cue Linköping, Sweden's Ghost.

I had heard Ghost's *Opus Eponymous* debut album on Rise Above Records back in early 2011 and it had impressed the hell out of me. Combining NWOBHM with Mercyful Fate, Cirith Ungol and Blue Oyster Cult meant it was a band tailor-made for my ears. But repeated listens left me unprepared for the first time I saw a photo of the band—a live shot of singer Papa Emeritus in full white regalia complete with an upside-down cross emblazoned on his mitre. I felt a jolt run through me, something I hadn't felt since I was a kid staring at KISS pictures thinking they were the greatest thing since sugar-coated breakfast cereals. And here was Ghost, a highly pronounced Satanic mélange of all the elements that made me fall in love with rock in the first place—loud abrasive guitars, daring costumes affixed with alter egos, tons of make-up and . . . Satan.

Just like toast without butter or fries without ketchup, rock music is dull and boring without Lucifer. With the beat, rhythm and moods rock stirs up originating from down below, he has every right to lay claim on it. Church people have been trying to tell us this for years and even though I outwardly laughed at their efforts to warn us, I knew too. The only difference was that I welcomed it!

These dark times we live in have only raised our threshold for extremes. It's permeated all aspects of our lives and rock music is no exception. I want my bands angrier, darker and more evil. Admittedly, KISS' once dark presentation seems a little lightweight to me now. Gene Simmons wearing a monster costume from 1976 now has limited cachet against bands who stopped flirting with evil and jumped in bed with it, head first.

I need Satanism in my music and I need a lot of it, only I don't want it presented to me in that hackneyed way of pathetic glumness, complete with upside-down frown and whimpering. I want disco balls and neon lights. I want sumptuosity and razzle-dazzle. I want a circus and the prom, a laser show and the Super Bowl all rolled into one from the moment the first guitar chord is struck. I want to be scared with sparkles and terrified with tremulous shimmers. And this happens the moment you put on Ghost's follow-up album, this year's *Infestissuman*.

Parental units like to thwart what they deem as diabolical activities, forgetting we were all weaned on ghost stories, Halloween and the monsters of *Sesame Street*. Adults unwittingly fostered these inclinations on my mind when I was young and it's too late and I'm too old to repress my attraction to the dark side now. Only now my tastes run a little finer. Papa Emeritus and his Nameless Ghouls meet these dark, sophisticated cravings flawlessly.

A version of this piece originally appeared Aug. 16, 2013 on the Huffington Post *website. Illustration by Eerie Von*

CHIP CUPS & THE SAD CASE OF THE COMMUNAL POTATO CHIP BAG

Being in a band has often been compared to being in a platonic marriage. You live and work with the same people for weeks, sometimes months at a time, eating and sleeping on top of one another in often cramped quarters. It can get quite hellish very fast and if one person doesn't get along with the others, a sort of Dante's 9th circle of torment ensues. It's no surprise then that bands switch members, go on hiatus, or simply break up as fast as they come up.

Sometimes the crux of the problem can be lain at the feet of simple personality issues. You can't get along with everybody. Often the reason people form bands in the first place is to publicly work on their obscene amount of personal issues. Contrary to the real world, rock 'n' roll can sometimes be seen as the last bastion where these flaws are celebrated. It's a place where someone doesn't need to ever grow up if they play their cards right. Public decorum, political correctness and social etiquette can all be happily replaced with vulgarity, gluttony and self-obsession in the coddled world of rock 'n' roll rebellion. Watching these types behave savagely might be enchanting from the sidelines, but having to deal with them when the curtain goes down, face-to-face, is a living nightmare.

In order to survive as a band, there needs to be a certain amount of mutual respect to go along with the instinctual "us against the world" rhetoric preached in the rock 'n' roll handbook. It's about more than letting the guitar player have a solo during the show; it's making sure you light a match after you take a shit in the one toilet the whole band is using for the next 24 hours. It's making sure you don't hog all the drinks on the rider. It's making sure you don't mow your buddy's lawn when it comes to women. A slight amount of respect is all that's needed and your band will last and last and last.

However, even when all parties involved are respectful of one another, a second tier of social rules develop that need to be maintained, or else they can threaten to rip the tightest of bands asunder. These evil, insidious little thought bubbles that burrow and nest in one's mind are known as "peeves." Yes, peeves, little causes of irritation. They can start off as benign as "I don't like this guy's hair," or "I don't like how he sips his drink," or "I don't like how he holds his fork," and it can fester into an all-out hate-on where you eventually threaten to burn his house down once the tour is over. I've watched many a band go up in smoke over peeves. You may call it petty or childish, but take a walk in these often worn shoes before casting the first stone. Even the most patient and saintly person will eventually reach the point where they're threatening to shank someone in the shower because they don't like how he/she ties their shoelaces. It's all in a day's work inside the rock 'n' roll circus.

So, how have I managed to come through unscathed after so many years? I haven't. Admittedly, I know all about this stuff because I've been on both ends. But I've managed to recognize this within myself and taken measures to keep those hurtful thoughts at bay. When they do eventually start to creep their way into the foreground of my mind, I take steps to turn it into a positive.

Here's an example of a recent issue where I made a mountain out of a molehill but managed to scale down:

In every band's dressing room there is what is known as a "hospitality rider," a certain amount of provisions requested by the band to make their stay more comfortable. This usually comes in the form of food and drinks, cups, plates, cutlery, towels, soap, etc. Some bands ask for lavish riders thinking it's all free and someone else is paying for it. We like to keep it stripped down and utilitarian—a few snacks, a few drinks and towels. Simple, right?

Not really.

All this is communal. The band and the crew, and sometimes the opening band and crew, are sharing our rider amongst ourselves. This is fine to a certain point. Drinks are individually consumed, so there's usually no issue. But food is another matter. Specifically, that communal bag of chips sitting on the table waiting to be eaten every time we walk into a dressing room. In fact, how people consume that bag of chips has weighed on me since I was a kid.

How the fuck does a party of two or more people consume a bag of chips together? My solution would be each person gets their own bag, but sadly this never occurs to anyone else. Most people open up the one bag and start shovelling chips in their mouth before passing it on to their friend while they watch television or drink beer and listen to tunes. Isn't this a form of double dipping? When you spoon a handful of chips and eat them, part of your fingers inevitably touch your mouth. You now have your own saliva on your fingers and if you go into the bag for another grab of potato chips you are transferring your saliva onto other chips inside the bag. Passing the bag over to your friend is now tantamount to french kissing them. This is fine when it's with someone you want to make out with, but definitely not fine if it is with someone where making out is simply not an option.

When you're out on the road, food can sometimes come at a premium. Starving bodies may sometimes throw decorum out the window, but it's still necessary to maintain civility. Watching someone pick at their teeth before throwing their hands into the potato chip bag forced me to come up with an easy solution to avoid having this scenario pop up at each show and become a divisive issue that would threaten the sanctity of our backstage environment and curtail any mental anguish on my part: Chip Cups.

Chip Cups are the solution to tight-ass, germ-averse snackers like me. Bowls are usually how one would keep chips outside of the bag, but at music venues bowls are often hard to come by. Cups (or glasses, if only available) are always easily accessible in any venue.

How this process works is simple. First, open the bag of chips. Make sure you're the person opening the bag to ensure it's an untouched, pristine bag. This also helps set a precedent. Pour a healthy amount of chips into a cup to show everyone that you have enough chips to allow others unmitigated access to the potato chip bag. Place the cup in the middle of the table for all to see and grab the cup when you want chips. Do not bring the cup to your lips like one would a drink. Rather, take chips from the cup like one would from a bowl. You have now established that this is the way to eat potato chips in this room.

This all may sound like a big deal for a non-problem, but you try having to perform with the image of someone else's saliva languishing on the caps of your teeth and the roof of your mouth. It's almost as if I can hear their DNA muttering to me, "you now have croup, salmonella, rickets, scurvy, chickenpox, gum disease . . ." while onstage. I know I would barely be able to breathe, let alone sing words. Whether people know it or not, the weight of a good performance rests on these fragile, piddling things.

All it takes is the one person to utilize the Chip Cup and everyone will follow suit, ensuring tasty snacks for all without having to taste whatever else was on the last guy's fingers.

Now, if that guy would only cough a different way or hold his coffee mug correctly or stop whistling every time he pees or use his left pocket to carry his cellphone or wear a better hat, I wouldn't have to whisper the phrase "Peace and tranquility is within me" a hundred times a day to keep from scalping him and forwarding spam to his email address when we get home from tour.

WHAT WOULD YOU DO? 20 QUESTIONS ABOUT ROCK 'N' ROLL

Since 2008, I've been posing ridiculous questions to *Close-Up Magazine* readers that sometimes test their morality, but mostly just question their fandom. Here are 20 of them:

1. You are sentenced to the electric chair. Your crime is not important. Friends decide to throw you a funeral service as well. What is the last song you wish to listen to before they pull the switch and what is the song you choose for your funeral service?

2. You are a failed guitar player that makes his living giving guitar lessons and painting houses. One day on the job, while refurbishing an abandoned house, you stumble upon a box of tapes that make up a long-lost Led Zeppelin album. It's an album that the band has completely forgotten about and no one knows even exists. If you were to play the songs to Jimmy Page or Robert Plant, they would have no recollection of recording them. Turns out, the album is easily the greatest Zeppelin record in their discography. You realize that if you were to record these songs as your

originals, it will yield you $500,000. If you turn it in, you will receive a finder's fee of $20,000, Jimmy Page's eternal gratitude and his deep lifelong friendship. What do you do?

3. You are the number-one Black Sabbath fan in the world. One day you decide to grow a handlebar moustache in tribute to Sabbath guitarist Tony Iommi and people immediately notice the uncanny resemblance. Furthermore, life suddenly becomes quite easy for you; people become friendlier, women become more attracted to you, and you start getting job promotions.

One day someone from the Sabbath camp spots you and invites you backstage to meet Iommi. Upon meeting you, Iommi appears visibly upset and is offended by your appearance. He impudently asks you to shave your moustache right then and there. Do you shave it off?

4. The year is 1990 and your favorite band, Guns N' Roses, are in the studio recording what is to become *Use Your Illusion I* and *Use Your Illusion II*. It's reported on the news that guitarist Slash has lost his signature top hat and there is a $10,000 reward for its safe return. You are dead broke but lucky for you, you've found Slash's hat.

Of course, you can't help but put the hat on just to see what it feels like. The moment you do a bolt of energy runs through your veins. You quickly realize that whatever skills you are already endowed with have been heightened; the report due on your boss' desk is delivered with high praise; your golf game rises exponentially.

Knowing that returning the hat would help your favourite band finish your two favourite albums, not to mention the 10 grand, do you still decide to return it?

5. You are a very successful Grammy-winning adult contemporary pop artist. One day you receive a special invite to the home of Paul McCartney. When you arrive at his house you are startled to discover that it's an intimate dinner made up of only a handful of special guests: his manager,

his daughter, his daughter's best friend, and Ringo Starr. During the dinner Paul McCartney tells you that he has recently written a song especially for you to record for your next record but wants no credit whatsoever. You agree to record the song despite the weird request and the night carries on until the early hours.

At around 4 a.m. everyone is quite inebriated and talk turns to classic Beatles stories. In a moment of impaired candor Ringo blurts out that the "real" Paul McCartney had indeed died back in 1969, a little after *Abbey Road* was recorded. He drunkenly continues on, (despite protests from the others to be quiet) and reveals that the other Beatles were shocked to discover this "new" Paul's innate musical abilities that allowed the secret conspiracy to continue, though it also was the reason for the break-up. Quickly sobering up, Paul takes you aside and confesses that Ringo's story is true.

Although he's not the Paul who played with the Beatles, he's still the Paul on the Wings albums and all "Paul McCartney" solo albums. Do you still record the song?

6. You are the biggest Robert Plant fan in the world. You own everything he's ever done and listen to him every day. As luck would have it, he moves into the apartment next door. At first you're over the moon and introduce yourself, but are surprised by his cold response.

As time passes, you notice that he doesn't become friendlier and is actually quite messy. He leaves his garbage out in the hall for someone else to pick up, almost like a hotel. You quietly clean up after him in order to keep the floor clean. He also stays up late into the night blaring opera music and singing at the top of his lungs. At first you enjoy listening, but as the months drag on you start to resent his blatant disregard for you and the other residents.

What puts it over the top is the odor that emanates from his place every time he cooks. It's a mixture of fish, dirty feet and rotten eggs. The smell is so strong it has permanently stunk up the whole floor and sometimes you can smell it wafting through your vents. Friends who come over think you smell and wonder if you're going crazy when you tell them it's actually Robert Plant.

Are you still a fan?

7. You somehow manage to sneak your way into an exclusive after-hours Hollywood party. The place is littered with beautiful, famous and important people. You manage to keep your cool and start effortlessly hobnobbing with other guests. Almost one after the other, you hit it off, not only with the supermodel of your dreams, but your favourite rock star of all time as well. Both are taken with you and each invite you back to their place. If you go with the model, you will have the best sex of your life and probably become her boyfriend. If you go with the rock star, you will jam his songs and probably join his band. Whom do you choose?

8. Your favourite band of all-time are at a crossroads. Their popularity has dipped over the years and many feel their next album might be their last. You have been asked to play lead guitar on this album. If you decide to play on it, you will forever be able to brag that you played on their record, which will give you a certain amount of prestige and a little bit of fame, but the record will be a dismal failure and end the band's career. If you decide to not play on the record, the band will become bigger than ever before. Knowing both these outcomes, what do you do?

9. You meet your favourite rock star backstage after a show. He is in full glory, holding court and entertaining a bevy of hot women. He's known to have a bit of a temper and doesn't like people criticizing him or telling him what to do. When you finally get your chance and approach him, you notice, dangling from his nose, a gigantic booger. No doubt, people have already noticed it but because of his volatile temper no one says anything. Do you tell him?

10. You are allowed to own either a gold record by Jimi Hendrix or the broken pieces from the guitar he famously lit on fire and destroyed at

the Isle Of Wight festival. If you choose the gold record, it's yours to keep. If you choose the broken guitar, you are not allowed to tell a soul and must keep it in a garbage bag down in your basement. If you do tell anyone, a mysterious man will immediately show up to your door, demand the guitar back and erase all memory of Jimi Hendrix ever existing in your world, including anyone you told. You must choose one or the other, which do you choose?

11. Mötley Crüe is your favourite band. You go see them in concert and when Tommy Lee throws his drumsticks into the crowd, one hits you square in the right eye. You are rushed to the hospital and are told that you have lost 70 per cent of your sight in your right eye. Your story makes national news. To your surprise you are visited by Tommy Lee and Nikki Sixx in the hospital. They manage to sneak you out and give you the best night of your life, hanging with beautiful girls, movie stars, rock stars and doing all kinds of drugs, all while treating you like their best friend. They offer you a chance to experience this for the rest of their tour as long as you don't sue them. If you decide to go on the tour it will be the best time of your life and you will remember it fondly forever. You'll also become lifelong friends with the band and part of their permanent entourage. If you decide to sue them you will be awarded $200,000. Which do you choose?

12. You are Yoko Ono's cleaning lady. You've been cleaning her place for years and years. During Christmas one year, Ono asks you into her study. As a Christmas gift she gives you a choice of taking either a brand-new, never-been-worn diamond ring worth $10,000 or you can take an old, very used handkerchief that belonged to Lennon but has been used by Ono for years. The handkerchief could fetch more than $500,000 or be worth $5. You are not a Beatles fan nor do you know anyone who is. Which do you take?

13. You have been asked to join either Judas Priest or Iron Maiden. If you

join Iron Maiden, you will be replacing Dave Murray. You will be in the band until they retire but you will never write any songs. Your job will be to play the songs live, essentially a hired gun. If you join Judas Priest, you will be replacing K.K. Downing. You will be in the band for one year but write the biggest hit they will ever have. You would become equally famous in either band and make the exact same amount of money. Which band do you join?

14. You have a choice of either the keys to the red ZZ Top car or the KISS Talisman set. If you choose the ZZ Top car keys, the car is yours for a day and you'll have 24 hours to right any wrong in your life. If you choose the KISS Talisman set, you'll be able to fly and have all the powers of each KISS member for a month. Which do you choose?

15. You are boarding an airplane headed to Tokyo, Japan, when you realize that Yngwie Malmsteen is on the same flight. You are a huge fan. He is sitting in first class while you are at the back of the plane in economy. You will never forgive yourself if you don't at least try to approach him and ask for an autograph. Hours into the flight you muster up enough courage and sneak into first class. As you are about to approach him, a woman pours her drink all over him causing him to throw a tantrum that awakens everybody because he's screaming "You've unleashed the fucking fury!" at the top of his lungs. If you do not ask for the autograph now, you will never get another chance to meet Malmsteen again and you will be detained upon arrival for trespassing into first class. If you do ask for the autograph, you too will become a target for Yngwie's rage but you may get the autograph in the end when he finally calms down. What do you do?

16. You are a struggling drummer with the clairvoyant ability to see people's real true potential. For example, if someone is pumping gas but could really become a great painter, you can watch their potential life unfold in front of you in a matter of minutes. However, if you mention

anything of this to them, their potential will immediately vanish. You can only watch from the sidelines to see if they find and fulfill this potential. Of course, there is always the huge possibility that they never find their true calling. All you know is that Eddie Van Halen is working as a dish-washer in Arizona, Slash is a roofer in Florida and James Hetfield is selling used cars in Rhode Island. It will take each of these three individuals at least 10 years to find their true calling and as long as you are nearby they will look to you to be on drums. On the other hand, they might not find their true calling and be stuck where they are for the rest of their lives. Which one do you choose to spend the next 10 years of your life with?

17. You run a small vending machine company. It makes you enough money to pay the bills and provide for your family. They're always break-ing down and you are constantly running around the city fixing them. One day, you pull up to a location only to find a guy smashing the shit out of your machine. He's screaming out loud, threatening to "kick its ass." It's obvious that the machine has been beaten beyond repair. When the assailant turns around, you notice that it's Kerry King of Slayer! Slayer is your favourite band of all-time. If you tell Kerry you own the machine he will start screaming at you, forcing you to defend yourself. Eventually you'll get financially compensated for the damaged machine, but you'll never see him again. If you start laughing and join Kerry in kicking your own machine you will become Kerry's new best friend, hang out with him for the day and be thanked on the next Slayer record, but never be compensated. Total damages would equal $5,000. How do you approach Kerry?

18. Tommy Thayer is out of KISS and you're in. You'll be playing lead guitar in one of the biggest rock bands in the world. The band has even given you a choice of either creating your own character with new make-up or adopting the Spaceman character. The night you get the gig, for kicks you decide to try on the make-up and quickly realize that you get

severe skin irritation. When the make-up is on, your entire face heats up and starts to burn and once it's taken off it gets extremely itchy. If you continue wearing the make-up day after day, your face will swell up into a bright patchy red. Swollen face or not, you look great when the make-up is on and you can play through the pain and irritation, so Gene and Paul are fine with it. However, your sensitive skin will make sure your life will be aggravating. Will you quit?

19. You arrive 10 minutes early to your appointed interview with Lou Reed at a five-star hotel. You decide to take a piss, so you walk into the hotel lobby washroom. When you open a toilet stall you realize Lou Reed is in there taking a shit and forgot to lock the door. You both make eye contact for at least 10 seconds—enough to remember each other's faces—before apologizing profusely, even calling him by name and wait outside the stall. When Reed emerges five minutes later you make a quick note that he never washed his hands! He was definitely taking a crap and he never washed his hands!

A few minutes later you are in his hotel suite and introduced to him by his publicist. Reed either doesn't remember running into you downstairs or is playing dumb. Either way, it makes it way less awkward until Reed holds out his hand for you to shake. Remember, he never washed his hands. What do you do?

20. You are on your honeymoon to Hawaii. On the flight from Los Angeles to Honolulu, you and your new wife get bumped up to first class. It's spacious and there isn't anybody there except Ozzy Osbourne! When you approach him and tell him how big a fan you are of his, he surprisingly invites you to sit down with him and begins regaling you with stories of the good 'ol days in Black Sabbath and making *Blizzard Of Oz*. Your wife, waiting for you to sit beside her, understands how much of a thrilling moment this is and quietly reads her book.

As Ozzy yammers away, you quickly notice that he doesn't just have a bad cold but is downright sick. Coughing and sneezing, he also seems to have a fever. Your quick summation leads you to believe he has a very contagious flu. You start to panic because you know that the longer you sit beside him, the greater your chances of getting sick in Hawaii and ruining your honeymoon. You also know that you probably won't ever get a chance to meet Ozzy again. If you stay, you'll get a bad flu and be left with a ruined honeymoon. Your wife will eventually catch it too and will be deemed unfit to fly home by the airline, costing you the return ticket, not to mention missing two weeks worth of pay at both your jobs. If you get up and leave Ozzy, you will have missed this once-in-a-lifetime opportunity with the Prince Of Darkness. What do you do?

Versions of these questions were serialized in issues of Close-Up Magazine *in 2008, 2010, 2012 and 2013.*

"OVERKILL" BY MOTÖRHEAD IS THE GREATEST ROCK SONG EVER WRITTEN

With the passing of Lemmy Kilmister on December 28, 2015, the rock 'n' roll world suffered a collective punch in the gut. In a community that exalts irreverence and rebellion above else, the outpouring of grief at his death spoke volumes. Lemmy was more than an unofficial king to us, his flock of black sheep; he was the icon, the role model, the blueprint.

Even now, only weeks after his death, he has already risen further in legend. Stories recounted by numerous people have already grown from tale to folk tale, from rock star to folk hero. He had so much charisma, so much personality, he merely had to flinch and one would walk away with their very own Lemmy story.

Literally overnight, the idea that we lived and walked the Earth during the same time Lemmy was alive has suddenly become surreal.

So now the time has come to evaluate just how much of an influence Lemmy and company had on popular music. With 22 studio albums under their belts, surely there's something beyond Lemmy's visual aesthetic and persona (black garb, distinguished cowboy hat, Jack & coke, long hair, custom-made boots) that made an impact, right? The first posit would be the song "Ace Of Spades," their signature song and means by which most people identify the band. While, yes, it's one of their greatest songs and one of the greatest rock songs ever written, they had an even better song, one that encapsulates the essence of rock 'n' roll—"Overkill."

The title track to the album released in 1979, "Overkill" clocks in at a lengthy five-plus minutes, meant to be more an album-cut than a catchy three-minute single like "Ace Of Spades" or "Iron Fist," despite its lead-off track status.

Lyrically, the song does little to go off script. One can easily dismiss its lyrics as another tired glorification of all things rock 'n' roll. Lines like "Only way to feel the noise is when it's good and loud" and "On your feet you feel the beat, it goes straight to your spine" aren't exactly poetic marvels, but that's the point.

And *that* "point" is so unmistakably found in the song's title— OVERKILL—defined as "excessive use, treatment, or action; too much of something." When it comes to rock 'n' roll, rules are turned on their heads. Terms like "progression," "exploring," "growing as an artist" and simply "artist," code words that give substance and gravity in other musical genres, are looked down upon as pretentious and laughable in rock. It's the conundrum of excess, redundancy and Dionysian delight wrapped within a simple framework that is the essence of rock 'n' roll, and "Overkill" by Motörhead is the best example of this.

The song itself is very simple, never veering from your standard box formation. It's this intangible quality that gives the song its breadth and life—a mélange of Lemmy's signature bass and vocal, Fast Eddie's wailing guitar, and the song's pièce de résistance, Philthy's drums.

If I am to proclaim "Overkill" as rock's greatest song, surely there needs to be a component of innovation and inventiveness. To this I would argue it's Philthy Phil "Animal" Taylor's double kick that drives the song, that brands it and accidentally creates the backbeat for an entire genre of music—thrash metal, which was also borrowed heavily by punk rock. The reason there are double kicks on drum kits all over the world can be traced back to this song and this song alone. Slayer albums wouldn't sound as explosive if for not this song. It would never have rained blood; it would've only rained.

But for me, the conclusive proof of the song's greatness lies with its ending. I have never heard a rock song that ends twice and "Overkill" ends thrice! On paper it would make no sense. In Motörhead's hands it's the only option to take, thus demonstrating the song's title and the music's meaning, all in one fell swoop. The arrangement ends at a comfortable 3:16 minutes, complete with customary crescendo, until it begins anew for almost another full minute before it repeats yet again. It's pointless, repetitive, obnoxious and absolutely perfect.

One must not misunderstand my take on "Overkill." My conclusions aren't based on sentimentality or nostalgia, but rather from a purely empirical vantage point. I've heard more than a few rock songs in my time. I've heard "Rock Around The Clock," "Hound Dog," "Paranoid," "Back In The U.S.S.R." and "Black Dog," but "Overkill" trumps them all. In fact, it's more than a song: it's the national anthem.

R.I.P. Lemmy Kilmister.

Danko Jones
January 20, 2016

A version of this piece was originally published in the March 2016 issue of Close-Up Magazine

Illustration by Richard Comely

ACKNOWLEDGEMENTS

Thank you to my patient and tolerant bandmates: JC and Rich Knox. They've heard all these opinions before in dressing rooms, vans, buses and even onstage.

Thank you to Duff McKagan for writing the foreword to this book. You are a prince, sir.

Thank you to Aaron Brophy and Ingrid Paulson for your expertise and patience. Thank you to everyone at Feral House.

Thanks to the illustrators whom I sought out for this book because I love their work: Gary Taxali, Mary Fleener, Gary Dumm, Damian Abraham, Valient Himself, Michel "Away" Langevin, Juan Montoya, Fiona Smyth, Cam Hayden, Eerie Von, Richard Comely and Brian Walsby.

Thanks to all the magazines and sites I've written for in the past and present: *Close-Up Magazine*, *Rock Zone* magazine, *Visions* magazine, *Rock Hard* magazine, *Rockstar* magazine, *Burning Guitars*, *New Noise*, *Guitar For The Practicing Musician*, *Metal Hammer UK*, *Mute* magazine and *Huffington Post*.

Thank you My Johansson, Reggie, Bjorn Barnekow, Josefin Fundin, Nick Sewell, Jonas Nilsson, Olle Burlin, Del James, Gordon Korman, Sean Yseult, Martin Svensson, Julia Holm, Götz Kühnemund, Robban Becirovic, Jonn Palmér Jeppsson, Jan Schwarzkamp, Jordi Meya, Devon Murphy, Danko Gabor, Ronny Bittner, Holger Stratmann, Dom Lawson, Scott Rowley, Sean Palmerston, Ronald Draijer, Sacrifice, Peter Pan Speedrock, Paul Bellini, Stuart Berman, Laura Dumm, Trisa Dayot, J.J. Dayot, Rick Schiralli and Mama & Papa Jones.

Thanks to our road crew: Corey Shields, Mathias "Stady" Stadlbauer, Andreas Skogmo, Tim Hughes, Magnus Tornqvist, Simon Follmann, Victor Marin, Biffen Jansson, Marko Harju, Fredrik Normark.

This book is for R. My records are your records.

DANKO JONES IS

the singer/guitarist of his eponymously named three-piece band.

DISCOGRAPHY:

Studio Albums

Born a Lion (2002)

We Sweat Blood (2003)

Sleep Is the Enemy (2006)

Never Too Loud (2008)

Below the Belt (2010)

Rock and Roll Is Black and Blue (2012)

Fire Music (2015)

Wild Cat (2017)

EPs

Danko Jones (1998)

My Love Is Bold (1999)

Mouth to Mouth (2011)

Compilations

I'm Alive and on Fire (2001)

B-Sides (2009)

This Is Danko Jones (2009)

Garage Rock! - A Collection of Lost Songs from 1996–1998 (2014)

DVDs

Sleep Is The Enemy: Live In Stockholm (2006)

Bring On The Mountain Documentary (2012)

Live At Wacken (2016)

BOOKS

Too Much Trouble: A Very Oral History Of Danko Jones, written by Stuart Berman, was released in 2012 by ECW Press.

I've Got Something To Say, written by Danko Jones, released in 2017.

He has also hosted his own podcast called *The Official Danko Jones Podcast* since 2011. It's available on iTunes and Soundcloud.

SOCIAL MEDIA

http://www.dankojones.com

https://www.facebook.com/dankojones/

https://www.instagram.com/danko_jones/

https://twitter.com/dankojones